The
Year
of the
Poet XII
February 2025

The Poetry Posse

inner child press, ltd.

'building bridges of cultural understanding'

The Poetry Posse 2025

Gail Weston Shazor

Shareef Abdur Rasheed

Teresa E. Gallion

hülya n. yılmaz

Noreen Snyder

Tzemin Ition Tsai

Elizabeth Esguerra Castillo

Jackie Davis Allen

Mutawaf Shaheed

Caroline 'Ceri' Nazareno

Ashok K. Bhargava

Alicja Maria Kuberska

Swapna Behera

Albert 'Infinite' Carrasco

Kimberly Burnham

Eliza Segiet

William S. Peters, Sr.

~ * ~

In order to maintain each poet's authentic voice, this volume has not undergone the scrutiny of editing. Please take time to indulge each contributor for their own creativity and aspirations to convey their uniqueness.

hülya n. yılmaz, Ph.D.
Director of Editing ~
Inner Child Press International

General Information

The Year of the Poet XII
February 2025 Edition

The Poetry Posse

1st Edition : 2025

Publisher Information

1st Edition : Inner Child Press
intouch@innerchildpress.com
www.innerchildpress.com

Copyright © 2025 : The Poetry Posse

ISBN-13 : 978-1-961498-55-6 (inner child press, ltd.)

$ 12.99

WHAT WOULD LIFE BE WITHOUT A LITTLE POETRY?

Dedication

This Book is dedicated to

Humanity, Peace & Poetry

the Power of the Pen

can effectuate change!

&

The Poetry Posse

past, present & future,

our Patrons and Readers &

the Spirit of our Everlasting Muse

In the darkness of my life
I heard the music
I danced . . .
and the Light appeared
and I dance

Janet P. Caldwell

Table of Contents

Curiosity, Fear, Loneliness

The Poetry Posse

Table of Contents . . . *continued*

February's Featured Poets   121

Inner Child Press News   151

Other Anthological Works   195

Foreword

Curiosity, Fear, Loneliness

It is a fact that shortened days, less daylight, colder weather and post-holiday stress can strike anyone during this time of year. To combat these feelings, we humans tend to make resolutions about how we are going to change. Often, by February, they have all fallen to the wayside.

The tendency to make amends to ourselves for perceived shortcomings often begins with the curiosity of where we could be. As we age, we experience life from a new world view. Sometimes that view is clouded by health issues, empty nesting and a lack of companionship from either death or breakups. The need to evaluate can move us toward a harsher than necessary assessment. The manifestation of our discontent is real, and pride may make us close ranks.

The fear of being discovered as lacking will keep one from healing. The ideal we have been existing under, in my case, for many years was simply a necessary smoke screen of contentment. It wasn't until I stepped away from that life that I was able to discover a new way of being. The fragility of a half life eroded all my visible edges. The ensuing loneliness of hiding myself from myself kept me from being all I am capable of.

Life is not easy; living is not easy. Find your curiosity of tomorrow and you can let go of the fear and the loneliness. Nothing lasts forever. The future is not finite. Our job is to create a tomorrow that we can welcome.

Gail Weston Shazor

Author, Poet, Humanitarian

Now Available

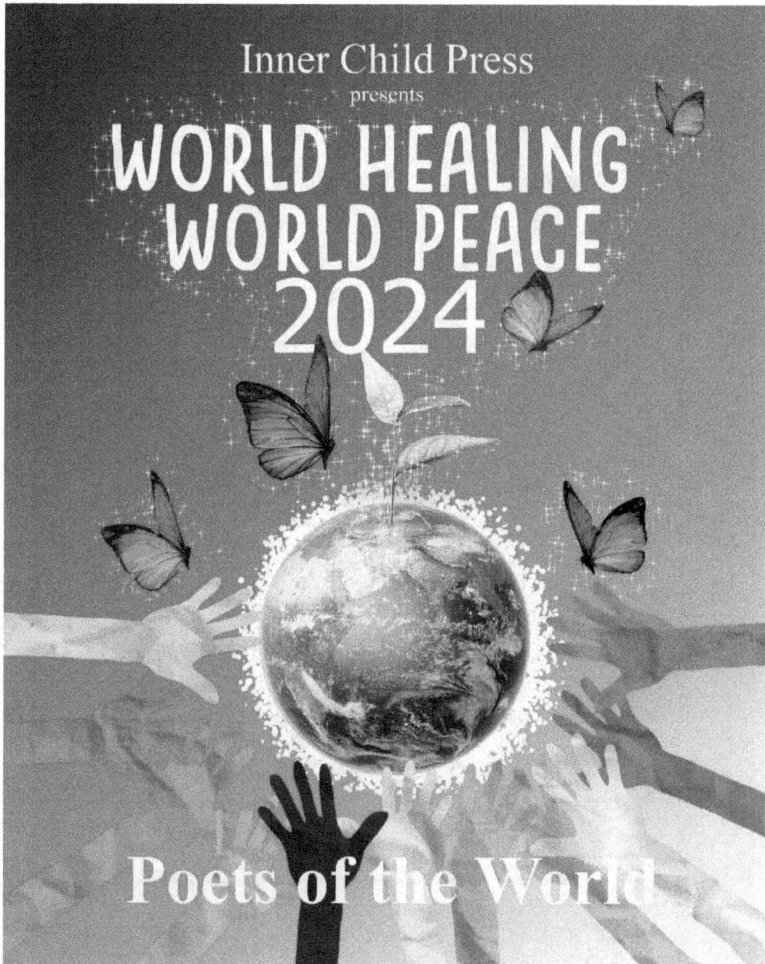

Inner Child Press
presents

WORLD HEALING
WORLD PEACE
2024

Poets of the World

www.innerchildpress.com/world-healing-
world-peace-poetry

Now Available

Preface

We, **Inner Child Press International, The Year of the Poet** and **The Poetry Posse** welcome you.

As we now have entered our 12ᵗʰ year of monthly publications for **The Year of the Poet**, we continue to be excited.

This particular year we have chosen to feature a collection of human emotions. We do hope you enjoy the poets perspectives on these subjects. Read ~ Learn.

For those of you who are not familiar with our story, back in 2013, a few of us poets got together with the simple intention of producing a book a month. That was our challenge. Since that time the enterprise has blossomed and brought forth a fruit that seems to keep on growing as evidenced as we enter 2023.

Our purpose is simple. Through our lyrical words and verse, we not only wish to share our poetic works, but we also have the poetic naiveté to believe that we can assist in the growth of consciousness of the things that have an effect our collective humanity. Therefore, we welcome your readership. For more about what we are attempting to accomplish, have a look at our Publishing Web Site . . . www.innerchildpress.com. If you would like to

know a bit more about this particular endeavor please stop by for a visit at :
www.innerchildpress.com/the-year-of-the-poet

Over the years, Inner Child Press has been socially active to bring awareness and catalog through literature the things that have an impact upon our world and its inhabitants. We have solicited, produced, underwritten and published quite a few volumes to that end. For more insight you may wish to visit : www.innerchildpress.com/the-anthology-market. If you are a writer, poet, or activist, you would be advised to keep a eye out for upcoming volumes should you desire to participate. All readers are welcomed as well. Note, that there is a myriad of published volumes that are available as a FREE PDF download as well as available for purchase at affordable prices.

We at this time extend to you our well wishes for your own personal journey and hope that you consider including us as a travel companion.

Bless Up

Bill

William S. Peters, Sr.

Publisher
Inner Child Press International
www.innerchildpress.com

Curiosity, Fear, Loneliness

Butterfly Weed   Hibiscus   Mimulus Aurantiacus

This month we focus on three themes: Curiosity, Fear, and Loneliness.

When I think of curiosity, I think of wonder, of our ability to see the wonders of the world and the terrible things in it and to be curious about how we can enjoy the miracles and help heal the rest. This month my curiosity led me to a TED talk where Irena Arslanova asks, "Does your heartbeat shape your sense of time?" Her research showed that each heartbeat momentarily suppressed perception, but that between the beats our perception of the world is increased. We can better understand our world when our heart is resting and we can better act or move when our heart is contracting. Our heart shapes how we see and participate in the world.

Poetry can have a positive impact on heart health by helping us process emotions, reduce stress, and improve our mood. Think about your heart as you read these poems. What draws you in? What raises your curiosity? What scares you?

The opening lines of Kahlil Gibran's poem "Fear" are "It is said that before entering the sea a river trembles with fear. She looks back at the path she has traveled, from the peaks of the mountains, ..." We all have fears. The question is what do our fears push us to do or prevent us from accomplishing? Sometimes our own fears and insights into other people's fears can garner compassion and a desire in us to help. What do you use your fear for?

The health care system reports the rise of loneliness, particularly in men. Studies and statistics show alarming rates, including only 27% of men having six close friends, down from 55% in 1995. Here we use poetry to express our own feelings of loneliness and other emotions. Sharing poetry, telling the truth about our lives, and listening to the stories of others are wonderful ways to decrease loneliness and increase heart health.

Kimberly Burnham

Spokane, Washington

Poets . . .
sowing seeds in the
Conscious Garden of Life,
that those who have yet to come
may enjoy the Flowers.

Poets, Writers . . . know that we are the enchanting magicians that nourishes the seeds of dreams and thoughts . . . it is our words that entice the hearts and minds of others to believe there is something grand about the possibilities that life has to offer and our words tease it forth into action . . . for you are the Poet, the Writer to whom the Gift of Words has been entrusted . . .

~ wsp

poetry is . . . .

Poetry succeeds where instruction fails.

~ wsp

Now Available

Gail Weston Shazor

Gail Weston Shazor is a lover of words. She is fond of the arcane, unusual and the not yet words.

Coining words at an early age, there was often a bit of trouble with teachers, but she always had her mother and aunt to back up her choices in expression. Born in Mississippi, she spent her early years with her grandparents. Each of the four left very careful influences on her pre-schooling. She learned in turn how women worked in and out of the home and how men worked in and out of the home to support the family. She learned that a lack of proper schooling was not the only way to learn and understanding life was a great teacher. As in most rural families of color, women had a greater chance of formal learning. Both of Gail's grandmothers read out loud to the family whether it was the bible or the newspapers and important documents to their spouses.

Gail Weston Shazor has authored (so far) Notes from the Blue Roof, A Overstanding of an Imperfect Love, HeartSongs and Lies My Grandfather's Told Me. The number of anthologies is too many to list with the premier accomplishment of one of the contributors to The Year of The Poet. Gail will always lend her ink to community projects and will purchase the books of fellow poets in the Inner Child Press family.

Goodbye

The mirror broke
I turned my head slowly toward the sound
Incomprehensible as it seemed
Unconsciously surreal
Not once had I given thought
To its possible insecurity

The air moved around my feet
The mirror broke
The old lady in the market might say
That someone in my house
Was about to die
But I live alone, you see
Still I gathered all the pieces
That I could sweep up
And put them in a cloth

The water is heading south
The air moved around my feet
The mirror broke
Carefully standing in the moving current
I lowered the cloth into the ocean
This is what a dawtah is supposed to do
I waited for the feeling to pass
That had begun in the kitchen
And moved slowly across my scalp

I swear I heard you sigh
The water is heading south
The air moved around my feet
The mirror broke
70 times seven you have been waiting
To leave this place
The wind has changed and your soul is released
I see you, moving towards home

4

Rescued

In the midst of this life
I find myself needing
To remember you
Pictures and words cannot replace
The feel of your hand in mine
And the feel of my heart
Echoing in your chest
For whatever reason the silvery thread
Of the fates unraveled
Into a rushing waterfall
Tumbling, buffeting and rushing
Me into disorientation
And when I would have clasped closer
You released your grip
I didn't understand the darkness
Until I was brought back into the light
I have caught my breath at last
After lying gasping on a far shore
And there are still days
That I cannot catch my breath
But they are no longer accompanied by pain
Instead, the joy is in the knowing
That it doesn't last for very long
And each new one is sweeter than the last
I have struggled with this for quite a while
The removing of the now for the want of happy
Each night I rest in prayer
That I understand the lesson fully
And yet I remain afraid to ask
If you still love me enough
For me to shod my feet once more
And for you to again become
My waking dawn and evening rest
At journey's end.

Death Has Spared Me Yet Again

Death has spared me over yet again
I do not think of death often
I plan my days for the next and the next
Without the thought that it is not promised
For in my small idea of humanity
I am not finished with the dreamtasks
I have stored in my head
And my 51 years are fortunate
The non-discriminatory timeframes
That border our waking and sleeping
Our rest and activity, our praying and praising

I do not think of death often
I wish to think that it doesn't think of me either
That somewhere the reaper is too busy
To give notion to my threads
And time keeps on moving
Whilst it attends to other tasks of fate
The words come heavy with dry breath
At the mention of death
As if any of us could escape notice
By only whispering its name
Without the fanfare that could draw attention
To what time we have remaining

I hold no notion that I will not die
And when I am forced to think on it
It is always with the thoughts of
Those I will leave to live without me
For even I know that death is for the living
The finality of the last breath
Does nothing for the breather
And the pain ceases with the end of mortality

On this day and in this week
Death has brushed by raising the hairs on my neck
And I realize that I am sad for me
Sad for everyone who feels the touch of ending
Old and young alike, freed from the bondage of dreams
From remembering what is was like to be near
The vibrancy of love and community
No one knows what will happen
Or even when it will happen
But because of this week, we know it will happen
Whether we do or do not think on death often

Gail Weston Shazor

Alicja Maria Kuberska

Alicja Maria Kuberska

Alicja Maria Kuberska – awarded Polish poetess, novelist, journalist, editor.

She is a member of the Polish Writers Associations in Warsaw, Poland and IWA Bogdani, Albania. She is also a member of directors' board of Soflay Literature Foundation, Our Poetry Archive (India) and Cultural Ambassador for Poland (Inner Child Press, USA)

Her poems have been published in numerous anthologies and magazines in : Poland, Czech Republic, Slovakia, Hungary,Ukraina, Belgium, Bulgaria, Albania, Spain, the UK, Italy, the USA, Canada, the UK, Argentina, Chile, Peru, Israel, Turkey, India, Uzbekistan, South Korea, Taiwan, China, Australia, South Africa, Zambia, Nigeria

She received two medals - the Nosside UNESCO Competition in Italy (2015) and European Academy of Science Arts and Letters in France (2017). Ahe also received a reward of international literary competition in Italy „ Tra le parole e 'elfinito" (2018). She was announced a poet of the 2017 year by Soflay Literature Foundation (2018).She also received : Bolesław Prus Prize Poland (2019), Culture Animator Poland (2019) and first prize Premio Internazionale di Poesia Poseidonia- Paestrum Italy (2019).

Curiosity

So many questions without answers.
Another discovery is a step forward.
I move slowly, blindly—
amid countless question marks.
I touch the great unknown.
A child still lives within me,
and I rediscover the world anew.
When I stop marvelling,
my mind will freeze like lava—
harden, lose its fire.
I don't want to forget
what wonder and awe mean,
the search for truth
and the rejection of old values.
I open the Akashic Chronicles.

Lost Data

I stand on an empty street.
The cold wind accompanies me,
tossing papers and bits of plastic carelessly.
Rain lashes my face and hands like a whip.
Dusk has awakened the windows of nearby houses.
They stare with hostile yellow eyes.
I'm not going home;
all addresses are strange to me.
Thoughts swirl in my head
like a startled flock of crows.
I remember nothing.
Fear grips my throat, choking me.
I belong to no one—
loneliness pulls me into nothingness.
I don't know my name or my roots,
where I'll find safe shelter.
My purse guardian of privacy,
remains silent.
I have no documents.
I have no money.
Keys shine, but to unknown doors.
I return from the void.
My recovered identity shouts my name aloud.
I push the nightmare out from under my eyelids.

Winter Landscape

I forgive you
for not appearing in my dreams
and for not meeting me in waking life.
In a land of leafless trees,
the cold whiteness of desolation
separates us.

Everyone has their own solitude.
Unspoken words die out,
losing their greenness
like unopened buds
withering on gray-brown

In my dreams, color appears.
Life awakens in the plant;
it wraps itself in celadon.
Hope, like revitalizing sap,
flows through my thoughts
with spring like vigour—
faster and faster.

Jackie Davis Allen

Jackie Davis Allen

Jackie Davis Allen, otherwise known as Jacqueline D. Allen or Jackie Allen, grew up in the Cumberland Mountains of Appalachia. As the next eldest daughter of a coal miner father and a stay at home mother, she was the first in her family to attend and graduate from college. Her siblings, in their own right, are accomplished, though she is the only one, to date, that has discovered the gift of writing.

Graduating from Radford University, with a Bachelor's of Science degree in Early Education, she taught in both public and private schools. For over a decade she taught private art classes to children both in her home and at a local Art and Framing Shop where she also sold her original soft sculptured Victorian dolls and original christening gowns.

She resides in northern Virginia with her husband, taking much needed get-aways to their mountain home near the Blue Ridge Mountains, a place that evokes memories of days spent growing up in the Appalachian Mountains.

A lover of hats, she has worn many. Following marriage to her college sweetheart, and as wife, mother, grandmother, teacher, tutor, artist, writer, poet and crafter, she is a lover of art and antiques, surrounding herself, always, with books, seeking to learn more.

In 2015 she authored *Looking for Rainbows, Poetry, Prose and Art*, and in 2017, *Dark Side of the Moon*. Both books of mostly narrative poetry were published by Inner Child Press and were edited by hulya n. yilmaz in 2019, *No Illusions. Through the Looking Glass*, which was nominated to be considered for a Pulitzer Prize by the publisher and editor of Inner Child Press, ltd.

http://www.innerchildpress.com/jackie-davis-allen.php
jackiedavisallen.com

Self-Reflection's Mirror

I can't breathe!
Is someone at the door?

From choices made out of anxiety,
one fear often outmatches another.
Alas, curiosity places on the back burner
a fear that fuels flames of misfortune.

But, what if innocence could prevail
and erase the mistakes
of youthful years,
would imagination tell truths
that sound like exaggerated tall-tales?
No way to back out,
no way to save face,
I'm not interested!
You all go on without me.
It's dark, the house quiet,
Whatever shall I do to pass the time,
until my family returns home?
It's Halloween, I'm eleven years old.
To myself, to God, I admit, I'm afraid.
The Fall Festival is not to my liking.
A skeleton, grape eyes, all laid out!
Entrails of noodles; blood-red, the wet-sauce.
Remembering my hands, my heart,
I'm unwilling to repeat fear's experience.

I'll stay home.
I'll hide in the closet.
My heart pounds loudly in my ears!

While There's Still Time

In the throes of life's darkest despair,
I revisit the acrimony swimming
around in my head. I flounder,
yet pay attention to that
which threatens to hold me hostage.

Devoid of the light, my life,
my safety is ebbing.

Into the darkness of night, like a moth
to the flame, I hover in pain.
In shame. Convicted of my weakness,
my need, I bow down in humility,
praying God's pardon.

See now how I wear my new name?
More appropriate, don't you think?

No longer do I dwell in remorse.
Nor do I stand in for so-called-friends.
Whose highs thrive on circular cliques,
that track shades of blame.
May my journey point yours to a new path.

What About the Others?

What said in haste, out of curiosity,
or in oversight, has become a blight.
Upon our friendship

Cleansed with tears
of remorse, you forgave generously.
And as always, hand in hand, we
attempted to follow a newer path.

I cannot help but think, despite the pain,
the awkwardness, that it has been worth it
The fences have fallen down.

The weeds pulled, and conversation,
has begun all over again.
With only a slight glimpse
into the infraction.

Would that the world be as forgiving,
as generous in its offering to others.
Let us follow the Golden Rule.

Tzemin
Ition
Tsai

Dr. Tzemin Ition Tsai comes from the Republic of China(Taiwan). In addition to being a professor of literature at a university, he is more committed to writing poems, novels, and proses. He is also an editor of "Reading, Writing and Teaching" academic text, an International editor of "Contemporary dialogues" literary periodical in Macedonia, and Vice-Chairman of the International Jury of the SAHITTO INTERNATIONAL AWARD in Bangladesh, and a columnist for "Chinese Language Monthly" in Taiwan.

In a wide range of literary creations, he is particularly fond of interesting stories or novels, and writing articles or poems about the feelings of nature and human beings. He has won many national literary awards. His literary works have been anthologized and published in books, journals, and newspapers in more than 55 countries and have been translated into more than 24 languages.

Autumn's Whisper, Eternal in Solitude

Neon reflections flow like water, counting moments lost.
An old man's shadow clings to the wall, murmuring to the
wind.
Since fallen leaves can cover the streets,
Why does no one remember the old poems when they are
scattered?
His steps press lightly upon fading echoes,
Each leaf carried away by unseen currents.
He bends low, gazing deep,
As though only now seeing yesterday's departure—never
to return.

Autumn wind floods the streets,
Its taste fills him, sweet as ripened persimmons, bitter as
passing years.
He fears being forgotten, like a fig tree barren in the
garden.
The television roars, a market of noise,
But a distant cat's cry strikes truer than all its clamor.
With solitude as his ink, he paints time into whispers,
Staring out toward the edges of fleeting days.

Standing in the dawn's pale light,
His gaze brushes the autumn song, still unweakened.
A faint smile graces his face, surrendering all to frost and
wind.
A child's laughter drifts past,
And fallen leaves dance freely in the breeze.
His soft sigh of dwindling years,
Rises far away, merging with the faint afterglow.
Of a starless, eternal sky.

Small Town Washed Away By Heavy Rain

Rain, caught off guard
Like the sky, still in the cracks that collapse silently.
The rain hits the tiles, and a piece of music sounds heavy,
Streets and alleys, rolling mud,
Erase them together, the shoe prints and the past.

At the entrance of the village, the old locust tree is bent in
the wind and rain.
It looks like an old man struggling to hold on to his roots.
The river is out of control and intends to swallow
everything along its shores.
On the river, the paper boat was left by the child,
Let the river be ravaged by the angry waves.

In the square in the center of the town, the water was up to
the knees,
People stood along the second-floor windows, spreading
mute prayers.
A broken umbrella that has lost its ability to compete with
the scorching summer heat, held by an old man,
Staggering, smiling in vain and dreaming, face covered
with frost.
Like holding, a lost and heart-burning memory.

Finally, the rain slowly stopped,
The sky was still gray, now as silent as washed plain cloth.
The alleys are paved with mud and broken branches, and
many heavy.
The little girl squatted by the river and picked up a piece of
soaked paper.
The boat she folded yesterday, now only vague traces
remain.

Meditations By The Hearth

In the wild grass, I sit, rain's whispers my companion,
While the riverbank loses itself in autumn's twilight hues.
The tides play their endless games,
Blurring the lines 'twixt sails and chimney smoke.
This lone stretch of water spans an eternal distance—
Can one small flask of warm wine ever rival the blaze of a
roaring hearth?
At midnight, I strike the chime of verse,
Seeking fleeting moments to return me to the days long
past.
But the tidings of my homeland—
Ah, how they tremble, elusive as ripples crossing the river's
restless waves.

After the rain, the skies clear, the window gleams bright.
The small pavilion warms by the embers' lingering glow.
The waning candle, still with vigor,
Yet my heart clings to the tender boughs once breaking
bud,
Bringing whispers of spring's first breath.
Now, I lie content amidst the lake and forest,
The silver strands of my beard unbothered by time's gentle
touch.
Ever do I pluck at blossoms' shadows,
Drunk with the kingfisher,
Together we fall into spring's verdant embrace.

Shareef Abdur Rasheed

Shareef Abdur Rasheed

Shareef Abdur-Rasheed, AKA Zakir Flo was born and raised in Brooklyn, New York. His education includes Brooklyn College, Suffolk County Community College and Makkah, Saudi Arabia. He is a Veteran of the Viet Nam era, where in 1969 he reverted to his now reverently embraced Islamic Faith. He is very active in the Islamic community and beyond with his teachings, activism and his humanity.

Shareef's spiritual expression comes through the persona of "Zakir Flo" . Zakir is Arabic for "To remind". Never silent, Shareef Abdur-Rasheed is always dropping science, love, consciousness and signs of the time in rhyme.

Shareef is the Patriarch of the Abdur-Rasheed Family with 9 Children (6 Sons and 3 Daughters) and 41 Grandchildren (24 Boys and 17 Girls).

For more information about Shareef, visit his personal FaceBook Page at :

https://www.facebook.com/shareef.abdurrasheed1
https://zakirflo.wordpress.com

What it is?

what me curious about
what makes folk tick
should i peak on the other
side of the fence
am i that lonely for human
contact considering how
folk act
is it fear of being alone
wanting someone to look in
on me to see how i be
still breathing maybe
humans love company
with humans who have humanity
is that the concern that generates
fear in me
so many who want to take advantage
possess poison baggage
be cautious about that
remember curiosity killed a cat

what judy said

don't piss on my leg
and tell me it's raining
never mind raining
it's urine flood mode
the bulls#i+ flows
folk in love with the
okye doke
so called leaders
blowing smoke
do i believe what i see
do i believe what i hear
dem out parading in their
underwear
here's the fact dem never
deliver what dem say
so the piss storm
on the radar is the norm
no wonder folk don't want
to hear the riff's
when dem always getting
stiffed

plots ' n ' plans..

hang around like pots ' n ' pans
doing all they can to mislead man
fooling fools, ignorance rules
they say " let's go and tell more lies
today. You know dem believe what
we say if we keep repeating it
everyday.
why we can control the flow what
we want dem to know
while twisting facts, stab truth in the
back,
dem consumed with hate based on
myths ' n ' fear
piss in dem ear
tell em what dem want to hear "
ignorance is bliss my dear
they lionize the criminal, vilify
righteousness
utilize subliminal try to frighten us
telling ya what's wrong is right for us
easy as going through butter with a
hot knife
is..,
stealing hearts ' n ' minds like a thief
in the night
left believing what their feeling instead
of facts proven right
bet if you come correct be ready to fight
because plots ' n ' plans doing all they
can to mislead man
all day. All night

Noreen Snyder

Noreen Ann Snyder has been writing since she was a teenager. She writes a variety of different topics. Her favorite poetic forms are Sonnets, Blitz, Haiku, Tanka, and Free Verse. She always learning different poetic forms.

Noreen Ann Snyder is a poet, writer, and an author of five books, (four books are co-authored with her late husband, Garry A. Snyder.) Her poetry is in several Inner Child Press Anthologies. She is the founder ofThe Poetry Club on Facebook.

A Lonely Child

I felt isolated and out of place
when we moved to Florida around 1968.
We were the new kids on the block.
Kids can be so cruel.
When the teacher stepped out of the classroom,
the boys would throw my lunchbox
like a football and laugh about it.
I was humiliated and in tears.
Kids made fun of me how
I talked and the clothes that I wore.
It's not my fault my dad and mom
made me wear these clothes.
Or how I talked.
I can't help it if I have problems saying
certain sounds or words.
It was a lonely life.
I felt invisible as if no one cared
growing up as a child and adolescent.
But I did survive through it all.
I no longer feel this way
I thank God.

Like the Fireworks

As I sit here alone on our front porch
watching and hearing the fireworks,
I think of you and I, our love.
Our love is like the fireworks
so powerful and beautiful.
Our love will stand the test of time
never wavering.
You make me feel that way.
We are proof that love can
be like the fireworks.

Make my Night

Where are you? You're supposed to grow old with me.

You didn't. I know you're in Heaven without pain

but still, I wanted you here at home pain-free m

love each other always and watch the rain

come down from the sky as we hold hands with glee

and do activities together again.

I want to love you, touch you, hold you, I plea.

Make my night, enter my dreams inside my brain.

Elizabeth E. Castillo

Elizabeth Esguerra Castillo is a multi-awarded and an Internationally-Published Contemporary Author/Poet and a Professional Writer / Creative Writer / Feature Writer / Journalist / Travel Writer from the Philippines. She has 2 published books, "Seasons of Emotions" (UK) and "Inner Reflections of the Muse", (USA). Elizabeth is also a co-author to more than 60 international anthologies in the USA, Canada, UK, Romania, India. She is a Contributing Editor of Inner Child Magazine, USA and an Advisory Board Member of Reflection Magazine, an international literary magazine. She is a member of the American Authors Association (AAA) and PEN International.

Web links:

Facebook Fan Page

https://free.facebook.com/ElizabethEsguerraCastillo

Google Plus

https://plus.google.com/u/0/+ElizabethCastillo

The Wandering Soul

In the depths of my soul, a fire burns bright,
A flame that flickers with curiosity's light
It beckons me to explore, to seek and to find,
The secrets that lie within the shadows of my
mind.

But fear, a dark and looming shadow, doth lurk
A specter that haunts me, a phantom that lurks,
It whispers of danger, of uncertainty and doubt
And tries to extinguish the flame that burns within
me out.

Yet, I cannot help but feel a sense of loneliness,
A longing for connection, for understanding and
for peace
For in the darkness of my heart, I find no solace,
No comfort to soothe the ache that doth never
cease.

So I wander, lost in thought and lost in time
A wanderer, seeking answers to the questions that
are mine,
And though the road ahead be fraught with fear
and doubt
I'll follow the call of curiosity, for it is my heart's
devout.

Whispers of Curiosity, Shadows of Fear

In the quiet corners of a mind that's keen,
Curiosity stirs softly, like the rustling of leaves,
With wide-eyed wonder, it beckons to explore
Unraveling mysteries that the heart believes.

It dances through the pages of forgotten lore,
Like a flickering candle in a cavernous night
Seeking the truths that lie buried in silence,
Each question sparkles, igniting the light.

But as the dawn breaks and shadows retreat,
Fear lingers close, a ghost on the breeze
A whisper of doubt that fills the vast void,
Binding the spirit, bringing it to its knees.

What if the journey reveals a hidden abyss?
What if the treasures are laden with chains?
The warmth of the sun seems so far away,
Lost in the echoes of unanswered refrains.

Loneliness wraps its arms, a cloak worn too tight,
In the silence of thoughts, where specters reside
While curiosity tugs at the heartstrings of hope,
Fear breathes its chill, like a tumultuous tide.

The winding path taken is fraught with the
unknown,

Yet every step forward is a leap of the brave,
To conquer the silence, to rise above fear
To face the tempest, to find what we crave.

In the depths of isolation, there's strength to be
found,
For solitude's whispers can lead us to grace
Though longing for connection often echoes aloud,
In the tapestry of life, we must find our place.

So let curiosity roam through the vastness of night,
Chasing the stars that once seemed out of reach
For even in shadows that thickly surround,
There lies a resilience that silence can teach.

Awakening the soul, a symphony played,
On the strings of the heart, interwoven with care
In the interplay of wonder and what holds us back,
A delicate dance, a fervent affair.

Embrace the uncertainty, for therein resides,
The magic of living, the spark of the new,
Each moment a canvas, awaiting the brush,
Where fear may retreat, and the spirit breaks
through.

Thus, in this delicate balance of light and of dark,
Where curiosity shines and fear finds its song,
We weave through the fabric of human despair,
Emerging through loneliness, resilient and strong.

Let the heart remain open, a beacon of hope,
Let the whispers of nature guide pathways we
seek,
For in the midst of the storm, as we venture alone,
We discover the strength to confront, to speak.

Through curiosity, we learn of each thread,
Through fear, we find courage to leap and to grow,
In the tapestry woven, each stitch tells our tale,
Of longing and finding, of ebbing and flow.

Here's to the dreamers, the wanderers bold,
To those who navigate the shadows we fear,
May curiosity ignite the pathways ahead,
For in every lonely corner, there's beauty held
dear.

In Quiet Shadows

In the cradle of dawn, where shadows blend,
Curiosity stirs, a soft, gentle friend.
With eyes wide as saucers, she tiptoes through
dreams,
Chasing whispers of knowledge, unraveling seams.

Through the corridors of thought, she wanders and
winds,
An insatiable spark in the labyrinth of minds.
What lies beyond the hills? What suns in the sky?
What stories are woven, just waiting to fly?

But lurking nearby is a specter—his name,
Is Fear, dressed in layers of shadows and shame.
He watches with silence, he breathes in the dark,
In the corners of vistas, he leaves his stark mark.

He stands tall and watchful, an ominous shade,
Concocting illusions, a masquerade.
"What if journeys lead to a treacherous fate?
What if the whispers are trickster's bait? "

Yet still, driven onward, Curiosity fights,
Through the fog of the unknown, towards
flickering lights.
In the heart of the storm, she reflects on her quest,
"Is it cowardice, or a yearning for rest? "

Loneliness drifts in, like a fog on the sea,
Caressing the edges of who I might be.
The echo of footsteps, the absence of voice,
In the stillness of night, where I long for a choice.

"Where are the souls who once roamed by my
side?
In laughter, in sorrow, in joy, we confide.
Now the silence is heavy, a weight on my chest,
In the vastness of solitude, I ache for the rest. "

Yet Curiosity rebels, breaks through the gloom,
With petals of wonder, she scatters the doom.
"Though alone I may feel, there's a world still to
explore,
In the depths of the forests, on the faraway shore. "

She climbs mountains of pages, of stories untold,
Finding friendship in words, and the solace they
hold.
For each line crafted gently, each stanza anew,
Is a bridge to connection, a tether or two.

Fear may rise like a tempest, with doubts to
bestow,
But Curiosity whispers, "There's more yet to
know. "
Loneliness, though present, does not have the
sway,
To quell the bright fire, to dim the sun's rays.

So dance in the twilight, where shadows converge,
With curiosity kindled, let wonder emerge.
For in the embrace of what dares to inquire,
We find threads of connection, and kindle the fire.

In the tapestry woven from fiber and thread,
Each question ignites, as new pathways are spread.
Curiosity, Fear, and Loneliness too,
Intertwined in a rhythm, the old and the new.

So let not the shadows consume all your light,
For in seeking, we flourish, expanding our sight.
Each whisper of knowledge, each heartbeat anew,
Turn the pages of life, with a vibrant hue.

In the end, they are partners—a dance in a ring,
Fear cautions the leaps, while Curiosity sings.
And even in loneliness, we find we're not lost,
For the quest to explore, is a treasure worth the
cost.

Mutawaf Shaheed

Mutawaf Shaheed

C. E. Shy has been writing since the seventh grade. He continued writing through high school, until he became more involved in sports. After his graduation, he worked at the White Motors Company where he wrote for the company's newspaper. He started a column called: "The Poet's Corner." That was his first published work.

www.innerchildpress.com/c-e-shy.php

Reading

It is hard to believe that there
will come a time when I won't
remember you or me or us.

That there will a complete
change in what was familiar.
Could it ever be I won't be
hungry for you?

That I won't be able to find you
even if I've exchanged eyes with
a hawk?

Will I never need you again, or
be in search of something, that
in my present state would be
considered un- delectable?

The possibility of there being no
more here no more now unsettles
me.

We may have to let go and
whisked away to a place called
there, where no time is present.

Where there is no need to count
numbers that don't exist.
Where is the music going to
come from now?

Maybe from the place it was sent?

Death Row Show

Sitting here on this planet waiting to be
granted a pardon from this place known
as death row. Don't know what time my
last phone call will go. Don't know what
my last meal will be. Why did someone
do this to me?

Dead planets surrounding me. I see, how
long I live isn't up to me. Rockets bombs
and planes have been responsible for my
gains. I think the aliens have lied to me.
Too many untrue stories have blinded me.

All the blood I shed , mixed some mud I
made, maybe I can create another sick
bastard like me? Hearing screams from
babies not too far away. Why should I care?
I live in cell block, USA. I don't care how I
really got where I am.

I'm trying to figure out how I can ride a
rocket or whatever else to get the hell out
of here. I don't think my imagination is
playing tricks on me. I've been holding the
other inmates in here at bay, Until I can find
how I'll get away. I can't go outside yet and
jump straight up!

Took a lot of fuel from fools. Plus, all of their
blood too. They know they what tell them it
all true . OOPS, another piece of space junk
has killed some more folks, only a few. That

device cost me 50 million bucks. I'd like to send
salutations from the furthest space station, to
the nation that help get away from them.

I'm still just outside the prison walls. Just be patient
I'll be right back to get all y'all! I plan to go visit
another prison across the milky way. I send back
some pictures via a radio waves, owned by me and
channel 23 someday.

Kiss Off

William tried to get in where he could fit in.
He really did belong near the top of the ladder.
He was smarter than all the suckers who were
there.

He had the wrong kind of hair.
The color of that skin he wouldn't blend in.
He had to freeze with all those degrees he
brought to the table.

He had to start at the bottom rung of the ladder,
 because they said someone gave those papers to him.
They set a suggestion box right next to where he worked
and said they would pay $50 for any thing that they would
use.

He got the message he wasn't a fool.
The suggestion he left them was written in bold letters.
When they opened the box they were aghast, the message
he
left them was kiss my degrees, all three. Then said good-
by!

hülya
n.
yılmaz

hülya n. yılmaz

Liberal Arts Professor Emerita, hülya n. yılmaz [sic] is Co-Chair and Director of Editing Services at Inner Child Press International, a published author, ghostwriter, and translator (EN, DE, and TU; in any direction). Her literary contributions appeared in a large number of national and international anthologies.

hülya writes creatively to attain and nourish a comprehensive awareness for and development of our humanity.

hülya n. yılmaz, a traveler on the journey called "life" . . .

Writing Web Site
https://hulyanyilmaz.com/

Editing Web Site
https://hulyasfreelancing.com

outside my home

i have never been an outdoors person,
appreciating nature's works from the comfort of my home
one day, i dared to leave my four walls,
venturing into what lay beyond
so, i encountered a first-timer in my backyard

"my" yard?
nothing about it was mine!

i sat on the lounge seat
and turned my head first toward the largest tree
i spotted something on one of its lower branches
and had to put on my glasses to identify it:
it was a hawk,
perched on one branch,
thus, not a daily sight!

my eyes opened wide
i surely was outside, mind you,
with my utterly enchanted insides

curiosity got to me
i got out of my chair,
slowly moving closer
to that stately presence

it was not at all intimidated by me
the merely few-feet-long divide
was for me a pure delight

i took several more steps in its direction
it slightly moved its head to face me,
while steadfastly staying at the border of "my" land

with childlike eyes, i kept eyeing the beautiful avian
on my path to approach it even more

what do they say? "Curiosity killed the cat."
thankfully, i was not one . . .

it rapidly flapped its wings
and began to fly
quite close to the ground

i am short, you see?
we, therefore, almost saw each other
eye-to-eye

it then took off into the sky,
leaving me, unharmed, behind

I Do

I fear fear itself

Unlike some who conquer it.

Could you tell me how?

emptied

three sets of ten years
breathing in merciless tears
unable to exhale

solitude, a steady companion
lives passing by
longing consenting to no passersby

but then . . .
sensation enters
your aged frame
attains its first-ever self-belief
your dried-up cells re-gain their womanhood
they wed your blazing passion, silenced since

heeding your longing psyche
after having starved it for long
you become one with your self

for a blissful while . . .

fast comes the instant to put to death
mercilessly your long-awaited reunion with the self

after the magical re-birth,
loneliness cannot lie anymore
for you had not ever been sated before
hence, the inconsolable aftermath

emptied

hülya n. yılmaz

Teresa E. Gallion

Teresa E. Gallion is a seeker on a journey to work on unfolding spiritually in this present lifetime. Writing is a spiritual exercise for Teresa. Her passions are traveling the world and hiking the mountain and desert landscapes of the western United States. Her journeys into nature are nurtured by the Sufi poets Rumi and Hafiz. The land is sacred ground and her spiritual temple where she goes for quiet reflection and contemplation. She has published five books: Walking Sacred Ground, Contemplation in the High Desert, Chasing Light, a finalist in the 2013 New Mexico/Arizona Book Awards, Scent of Love, a finalist in the 2021 New Mexico/Arizona Book Awards and Come Egypt in 2024. She has two CDs, *On the Wings of the Wind* and *Poems from Chasing Light*. Her work has appeared in numerous journals and anthologies.

Website: http://teresagallion.yolasite.com/

Loneliness is Not an Option

Loneliness is not an option
floating down an ancient river,
nor breathing the succulent air
flowing from a mountain vista.

Loneliness is not an option
when walking a soft needle trail
in the ponderosa forest.

Loneliness is not an option
when gratitude overflows in the heart
and mist from a waterfall
sprays you with love.

Loneliness is not an option
when the lonely road of regret
tries hard to grab your soul.

Loneliness is not an option.
I resist with the force of love
from the Beloved's gaze.
Resilence harbors in my bones.

Curiosity is Bold

Curiosity is a never-ending spark.
It pushes us to grow
and expand our horizons.

It opens the windows
that cover our eyes
and light floods into our brains.

We cannot resist the call
to seek out meanings
floating on rainbows.

We chase the embers
running in the wind.
There is hope for a landing
on the star of our dreams.

The Tao of Light

Do not be jealous of your happiness.
There is an ecstatic mountain
that wants to nourish your soul.
You need to go there.

Start your walk at daybreak
when radiance hugs the ground.
Walk slowly between light streams.

Do not be swayed by judgmental stones.
Stay focused on your ascent.
There is a bucket overflowing with joy.
It waits patiently to merge with you.

Stay open to an endless possibility of bliss.
The brighter the light shines,
the more pleasure you will feel.

Walk back down the mountain.
Smile at all homo sapiens.
They will stare in awe at your glow
and know not why.

Ashok K. Bhargava

Ashok Bhargava is a poet, writer, inspirational speaker and a literary consultant. He has attended poetry conferences in Italy, Turkey, India and Philippines. His latest book "Riding the Tide" about his battle with cancer has been translated and published in Arabic, Hindi, Telugu and Bengali languages. He is a contributing writer to several anthologies worldwide including World Poetry Almanac 2014. He has been published in numerous print and online magazines.

Ashok has won many accolades including Poet Ambassador to Japan, Kalidasa International award, World Poetry Lifetime Achievement award, Writers Beyond Borders Peace award and Tapsilog Leadership award for his community involvement. He is founder of Writers International Network Canada Society to discover, nourish, recognize and celebrate writers, poets and artists and to assist them to network with the community at large. He is the author of eight books of poetry and one anthology. He is Artist-in-Residence at Moberly Arts & Cultural Centre and also co-edits the literary section of The Link Newspaper.

Flashes of Loneliness

"The beauty and brutality of family relationships comes in many forms like splashing waves and tides".

Relations can't hold balance
if gravity shifts
abruptly.

We know how a falling tide
leaves a coral reef
exposed to emotional bleaching.

Treasures
found only
in the calm sea.

Counting pitfalls of others
a thousand times won't
change the past.

Sometimes a breath is just a breath
sometimes it sustains
everything.

Let's wring more out of the time
that is left
to live.

Bonded Forever

He sped away in his car
Leaving behind shattered feelings.

Shocked
I didn't know where to go.

My trembling voice asks
'What will happen now'.

I say to myself
Perhaps it's the end.

Is our DNA knotted together
Or could we be untied.

I see the full moon
Guide me towards light.

I gather the fragmented emotions
Glue them together.

Dazzling kaleidoscopic
Hopes emerge, it's not over yet.

Silent Crossroads

I feel hopeful
I wait for change
But it misses me.

Whatever I have been
I remain.
It's just another day.

No response.
No sign.
I remain silent.

I become sigh
In the long unending nights
Feeling your voice.

I can't tell you what to do.
I control only
What I could say.

I can't come to meet you but express
Only my enduring love for you
My poetic sermons.

Meanwhile a young boy
Dreams and waits
For his grandparents.

Caroline
'Ceri Naz'
Nazareno
Gabis

Caroline 'Ceri' Nazareno-Gabis

Caroline 'Ceri Naz' Nazareno-Gabis, author of Velvet Passions of Calibrated Quarks, World Poetry Canada International Director to Philippines is a multi-awarded poet, editor, journalist, educator, peace and women's advocate. She believes that learning other's language and culture is a doorway to wisdom.

Among her poetic belts include **Gabrielle Galloni Memorial Panorama International Youth Award 2022**, Panorama Youth Literary Awards 2020, 7th Prize Winner in the 19th, 20th and 21st Italian Award of Literary Festival; Writers International Network-Canada ''Amazing Poet 2015'', The Frang Bardhi Literary Prize 2014 (Albania), Poet Journalist Award 2014 (Tuzla, Istanbul, Turkey) and World Poetry Empowered Poet 2013 (Vancouver, Canada). She's a featured member of Association of Women's Rights and Development (AWID), The Poetry Posse, Galaktika Poetike, Asia Pacific Writers and Translators (APWT), Axlepino and Anacbanua. Her poetry and children's stories have been featured in different anthologies and magazines worldwide.

Links to her works:

http://panitikan.ph/2018/03/30/caroline-nazareno-gabis/

https://apwriters.org/author/ceri_naz/

http://www.aveviajera.org/nacionesunidasdelasletras/id1181.html

When Curiosity Sparks

When the world was made in a grand design

Hidden truths were quiet,

So questions asked the mind

A relentless journey for answers keeps going,

When the flame of curiosity upbeats,

Chasing rainbows of meanings are confined,

As we explore the causes and effects

Life becomes an open book of quest,

Where wisdom weaves and sees us through

We learn, thrive, and survive,

Driving progress all along,

As we aspire to shine,

The fire of knowing comes alive.

Why Fear Visits Me?

I didn't know about this secret friend
Visiting me and whispers
The shadows presence that make me tremble
And my body reacts in the unknown halls.
In the stillness of the night,
It drives me frozen, sometimes unbidden ghost bumps
Creeping to my senses.
Every heartbeat,
Ascending shivers,
Revealing harsh pricks
But I couldn't catch it,
I just told myself,
Master the courage
In this dark carousel,
Binding my mind,
To my soul.
I learned as I grew,
The moment this feeling comes in
I think of the blaze of the sun,
To melt the icebergs of fear,
 Transform the thumping, cracking rocks
Into the ocean of calmness,
Here in my heart.

Don't Make Me Lonely

Don't make me lonely,
Sometimes, I need your touch
From the wilderness, I cry,
I seek those arms to caress me,
In the vast expanse of time and space,
I want to hear your voice
To lift my heavy load
Beneath the echoes of stormy tides,
Don't make me lonely,
I need your presence, may this feeling subside.
I can hear your laughter etched in every wall,
I lost you in my dream,
My fragile heart needs the constant song,
You're so distant for me to hold,
Hoping tomorrow will paint a smile,
In your warmth, I wish to stay forever,
Don't make me fall, don't make me lonely,
From these chains of tears and downhills' story
In your warmth, I wish to stay.

Swapna Behera

Swapna Behera is a trilingual poet, translator, environmentalist, editor from India and author of seven books of different genres including one on children's literature on Environment. She is the recipient of International UGADI AWARD 2019, honoured from Gujurat Sahitya Akademi 2022, 2021 International Poesis Award of Honor as Jury, Pentasi B World Fellow Poet, Honoured Poet of India from Seychelles Government and International awards from Algeria, Morocco, Kajhakhstan, modern Arabic Literary Renaissance of Egypt, International Arts Council Argentina etc. Her stories, poems, articles are published in many International and National magazines and ezines. Her poem A NIGHT IN THE REFUGEE CAMP is translated into 67 languages. She has received over 60 National and International Awards. At present she is the Cultural Ambassador for India and South Asia of Inner Child and the life member of Odisha Environmental Society

Email
swapna.behera@gmail.com

Web Site
http://swapnabehera.in/

The child with the mask

"Curiosity is more important than knowledge" -Albert
Einstein

The child with the mask
Pondering over a task
Thinking millions why,
With a wooden wand

Peeps behind the paper
Dreams with the nature
Bright Colours of life
Dazzles on the road

Why the frog eats the bug
sweet toffee mother's hug
Why the cow never says
Good morning, Good bye

Why the money makes the story
And the milk sings the Lori
Why the blood flows on the road
When the people fight and fight

Why the honey tastes so sweet
red eyes so bitterly tweet
Why the people run and run
Never smile for a year?

Echo of the Epicentre

The sizzling voice from the epicentre whispers---
May I earn a smile???
A smile that gives a choice,
Choice to live and love,
fly or swim,
earn fame and never a sham
put on the dawn, and never a dusk

Choice to be pregnant or to be my own self,
lend my skill or express my agony,
Choice to be secured,
And vibrate my ambition and desires,
Choice to be a virgin or a mother,
My existence is the thunder of the Nature
I am not a slave-

A slave of rituals, superstitions,
Fanaticism and vandalism
My womb is never ever for bloodshed
The uterus that creates
and never destroys -
You may dig a pit
Keep me underground
You may burn my wax clad,
Or dissect my flesh and blood
Still then----

I am a wonder woman
 a thunder woman
My tears and blood will write
The epitaph of kindness
I am the lady with the lamp
Healing in the battle field

May I earn a smile??
May I be surrogated
with peace and love
For ever and ever??

And They Say ---

"Extreme fear can neither fight nor fly" – William
Shakespeare

And they say
Fear is in the air !!!
Fear that chains the feet of the women
Fear that rapes her identity
Fear that brings tears to the orphans
Crushes the creativity
Crumbles the teens
Stumbles in hunger
Covers her existence with a hijab
converts her highway into a cemetery

May I ask you dear fear???
Can you dissolve her soul?
Can you melt her blood?
blood that knows the worth of bloodshed--
She is never a lonely star dear
She can encounter billions of fears
She has multiple identities,
Roles on stages of life
Roles that scribble in the horizon
To teach and enrich self and all
She is an existence, an ocean of love
a healer - the cosmic transmitter
She is the soul of Draupadi
reborn as Phoenix with honour and valour
She is in the smile of Peace- the shield against bullets
She never sleeps or ever envies
the blanket on the beggar
The hallmark of love
chorus of truth that dances with all

Swapna Behera

The luminous valley waits for her
Where the cuckoo sings,
the grass dazzles
the fragrances intoxicate
From here to there --
From you to you
From one to millions

Albert 'Infinite' Carrasco

Albert "Infinite The Poet" Carrasco is an urban poet, mentor and public speaker.

Albert believes his experience of growing up in poverty, dealing with drugs and witnessing murder over and over were lessons learnt, in order to gain knowledge to teach. Albert's harsh reality and honesty is a powerfully packed punch delivered through rhyme. Infinite grew up in the east part of the Bronx and still resides there, so he knows many young men will follow the same dark path he followed looking for change. The life of crime should never be an option to being poor but it is, very often.

Infinite poetry @lulu.com

Alcarrasco2 on YouTube

Infinite the poet on reverbnation

Infinite Poetry

www.lulu.com/us/en/shop/al-infinite-carrasco/infinite-poetry/paperback/product-21040240.html

www.innerchildpress.com/albert-carrasco

Loneliness

My worse fear is loneliness. I know I was born alone and that I'll die alone, but while I'm here

I want to be a familiar face and not roam this sphere as an unknown. Loving hard is my specialty, no matter how hard life was for me, i spread love unsparingly rather than dwelling in misery. I've gained this fear due to losing a lot of sisters and brothers from everything from cancer to murder, it started when i was just twelve years old. That's the age I was, when I lost my father. I was young and dumb, i thought he'll come back, but I quickly realized that wasn't a fact, since then I've dealt with death back to back. I always wondered when it would end but it hasn't. Not even a year ago i had to say bye to a childhood friend. I've prayed and prayed… God please spare my love ones. I know what's written can not be erased, but can you please slow down time so i can spend more time with people that can never be replaced. Losing so many loved one hurts, it's and indescribable pain to have to follow hearse after hearse like a mourning train where tears fall like black cloud rain. There was times when i wished i was the first to go to heaven, rather than to feel the loneliness from the aftermath of disease deterioration and gun powder detonations. To everybody out there please hear me, when i say please don't leave me. I need you.

Sick

I'm so ill wit it they say there's no cure, "The eight spits so sick his bars surpass stage four",

I've been blessed to avoid death so I can grab mics and asphyxiate em till I take my last breath, I had a band of brothers but the fat lady ruined the orchestra singing bloody murder over and over, caskets closed like curtains till I became one of the last of the original members left.

Soul theft was a part of a game we played, we might of lived blasphemous but we prayed just like those with religion, we weren't atheist, we knew there was a higher power but we just considered ourselves Gods forgotten children. Living in hell it's hard to maintain hope so we sell or abuse to cope, we figured if we made fast money we could relocate or if we got higher and higher we could speak to Angels as we levitate.

Unfortunately a lot of men didn't get the opportunity for relocation, going from hell to heaven was their only transition. The game scarred me, I'm full of keloids internally and I have a few externally from slugs going in and out of me, the pain I've felt and was forced to see all was a prelude to my urban poetry and it's potency. I'll hit ya with NYCHA property prophecies, I'll keep it one hundred percent real and say that I've seen men get rich from the game, pockets heavy pushn beamers, benz and Bentleys, but I've seen so much more needing to be morgue I'd'd. If the reaper didn't get em the feds did and gave em life in the system.

The odds of survival are slim, if they're not dead or in jail they're out here with me witnessing evolution. Seeing a familiar face from the days of do-g and bass is rare, when I pass thru old blocks there's new dudes yelling out stamps and colors into the air. They're the new gen hustling hard to end poverty and live a good life, unfortunately they don't know history is going to repeat on these old blocks, today they're hot, tomorrow they'll be cold as ice. In the game early death is the usual fate and it correlates with bidding with no release date. I overstand that I can't change what is written but I also overstand that I can write to make change.

Short stay

We are not the same, I'm him, I pull up to pick up my lady playing surface because I want to let her know that she's my everything, but I don't sing. See I'm an old school brother, in the summer I'll throw on sweats or shorts with a wife B and a white T or light linen in all colors, in the winter it's denim or butta leather accented with anything from slippers, j's, timbs to Gucci loafers depending on the weather. The whips aroma will be from an entourage wrapped around green flowers mixed with the scent of vanillaroma, windows up, roof closed, if you know you know I stay in a chamber like a slug ready for danger, pockets are full of paper so we can do anything anywhere at anytime, I mean whatever. We can cruise New York and do what we do as native New Yorkers, or I can pull up to Kennedy or LaGuardia to go somewhere to get another stamp on our passports, so we can sit under palm trees and swim in the clearest blue water and spend a night on the beach sippn top shelf as we enjoy each other… till the next day, the sand is my Telly… that's what I call a short stay.

Kimberly
Burnham

A brain health expert (PhD in Integrative Medicine) and award-winning poet, Kimberly Burnham lives with her wife and family in Spokane, Washington. Kim speaks extensively on peace, brain health, and *"Awakenings: Peace Dictionary, Language and the Mind, a Daily Brain Health Program."* She recently published *"Heschel and King Marching to Montgomery A Jewish Guide to Judeo-Tamarian Imagery."* Currently work includes *"Call and Response To Maya Stein an Anthology of Wild Writing"* and a how-to non-fiction book, *"Using Ekphrastic Fiction Writing and Poetry to Create Interest and Promote Artists, Writers, and Poets."*

Follow her at https://amzn.to/4fcWnRB

Curiosities and Questions for a Puppy

Why do puppies get the zoomies
why do they chew on shoes
when there is a house full of chew toys

Why does my heart open in just a few days
to love an animal I didn't know existed
until I brought her home

What do the other dogs think about
when they bark and sometimes
snarl at her when she gets too close
leaping and bouncing full of energy
then a few days later
curl up on the bed with her
all snuggled up next to me

What flips the switch when she knows
to use the dog door to go outside
not chew on shoes
keep her teeth to herself
give the goats a wide berth
and leave the 14-year-old cat alone
with just an occasional lick to his head

Why do human beings abandon puppies
leaving them to fend for themselves
like wild animals in the cold
dropping them for someone else to find
starving and take to an animal shelter

Dendrophobia: The Fear of Trees
after Fear, Kahlil Gibran

Does a Japanese maple tree fear losing her leaves
is she jealous of pines' all winter green
looking down as the colors fade
from bright reds, oranges and yellows
to a muddy brown

Does the pine fear the fire
wishing instead he had been cut down
cleared away before the dry winds
blew in hungry sparks seeking wood

Do the winds regret their part in fires
wishing instead they could pick up moisture
from the ocean, from lakes and rivers
carrying it to parched lands
a blessing desired by all

Does the water try to find its way
to all parts of the land and the forests
or does it play favorites
watching from a far as trees lose their leaves
kindling for the fires' rage

Does the fire regret avarice
a greedy obsession gobbling more and
more till all is consumed
as the barren land draws speculators
profiteers looking for ways to benefit
from destruction

Causing dendrophobia
the fear of trees in homeowners

stuck in one location able only to move
what fits in their cars wishing
they had cut down all the trees
cleared the land, created a desert
around their house leaving the flames
nothing to burn

Preferring One Religion Over Another

I prefer one religion over another
in America I can choose where and whether I go
to services and how I practice
my beliefs and connection to the universe

I prefer to do it my way
I am free to roam the streets
to drive to a synagogue
or a temple or a church
for whatever events I want

But I am not always safe
the streets and neighborhoods
where I walk are sometimes filled
with hate against me because of how I choose
to see the universe here in America

Nonetheless, I am free
I do not sit on death row in Alabama
I am not a mother with a baby in her womb
wrapped in my freedom I wonder
why every person does not have the right
the freedom to practice as we wish
letting others do the same

Eliza Segiet

Eliza Segiet graduated with a Master's Degree in Philosophy at Jagiellonian University.

Received *Global Literature Guardian Award* – from Motivational Strips, World Nations Writers Union and Union Hispanomundial De Escritores (UHE) 2018.

Nominated for the Pushcart Prize 2019, 2021.

Laureate *Naji Naaman Literary Prize 2020,*

International Award Paragon of Hope (2020),

World Award 2020 *Cesar Vallejo* for Literary Excellence. Laureate of the Special Jury *Sahitto International Award* 2021, World Award *Premiul Fănuş Neagu* 2021.

Finalist *Golden Aster Book* World Literary Prize 2020, *Mili Dueli* 2022, Voci nel deserto 2022.

At the international Festival of Poetry CAMPIONATO MONDIALE DI POESIA (2021/2022) she won the title of vice-champion of the world.

Award BHARAT RATNA RABINDRANATH TAGORE INTERNATIONAL AWARD (2022).

Award - *World Poets Association* (2023).

Laureate Between words and infinity *"International Literary Award (2023).*

Pretending

He was discovering the world
even through a keyhole.
He saw fascinating
– seemingly inaccessible –
crystals of life.

When he realized
that even the real Santa Claus did not exist,
he stayed silent!

Sometimes it's worth pretending
that we don't know
what we do know.

Translated by Dorota Stępińska

Everyday Life Shuttered

It could not have been predicted before
that somewhere far away,
across the ocean,
before the eyes of billions,
a dreamed-up world would bleed out –
turn into a kingdom of death.

In disbelief,
he stared at the TV screen.

A plane, a building, smoke, dust,
another plane...
There were also people! That's what mattered most!
They were trying to save lives, not only their own.

Until the day that began as
a seemingly ordinary September morning,
he had not known what fear was.
Now he did!

He understood
– it was not fiction.
Everyday life that shuttered
ruins the world.

Translated by Dorota Stępińska

Masks

Thoughts swarmed
about the possibility of change.
They grew cold when he realized
that loneliness was a creation of the mind.

He stopped seeking friendship
for better or for worse.
He now knew
that disappointment awakens
the desire to try again.
He instilled in himself the certainty
that one day,
unexpectedly, he would emerge from the darkness
and there would be light.
He no longer went out
– like Diogenes had once done –
with a lantern in search of a man.
The path he might have walked
was already covered with moss.

Under the sloping,
wavy roof of his own house,
between the pages of a dusty book –
he discovered wisdom carved in stone,
words that would not disappear.

Engrossed in reading, he found companionship,
loneliness became a thing of the past.
There he found dilemmas similar
to those he had experienced,
but –
also an invisible clarity of mind.

Being yourself
– is not to wear masks.

William S. Peters Sr.

William S. Peters, Sr.

Bill's writing career spans a period of well over 50 years. Being first Published in 1972, Bill has since went on to Author in excess of 50+ additional Volumes of Poetry, Short Stories, etc., expressing his thoughts on matters of the Heart, Spirit, Consciousness and Humanity. His primary focus is that of Love, Peace and Understanding!

Bill says . . .

I have always likened Life to that of a Garden. So, for me, Life is simply about the Seeds we Sow and Nourish. All things we "Think and Do", will "Be" Cause and eventually manifest itself to being an "Effect" within our own personal "Existences" and "Experiences" . . . whether it be Fruit, Flowers, Weeds or Barren Landscapes! Bill highly regards the Fruits of his Labor and wishes that everyone would thus go on to plant "Lovely" Seeds on "Good Ground" in their own Gardens of Life!

to connect with Bill, he is all things Inner Child

www.iaminnerchild.com

Personal Web Site

www.iamjustbill.com

Curiosity, fear and loneliness

Curiosity leads to exploration
For many of us   . . .
For others it leads to a fear of the unknown
Which at times
Consumes us

Are not we all lonely
At some segment of
Our lives . . .
Yet my curiosity prevails
As I wonder what could be
If I allow my sails
To capture the wind

No Sense

The emptiness at times
Overwhelms me,
But i fight back

My favorite defence
Against self-reconciliation
Is to increase the noise
And indulge in the inner chatter,
When I do know that
Silence is the objective
My soul seeks

There is an abiding fear
We all have
Of loneliness
Or abandonment,
For who amongst us
Would shun an earnest embrace
Where the warmth is
Authentic and sincere?

I was invited to dinner,
But i could not find the seat
That fit me best,
So I drank from
The empty cup before me.
.....
The offered liquid was wet
But it did not whet my senses,
Nor was my thirst abated,
For i had a different
Type of need,
That only my soul knew of.

I felt empty,
Yet full of the 'bull'
That gave cause
For my skull to hurt
As i attempted to skirt the issues
That were sucking me into
The quagmire
Where all my pains,
Ills, fears and doubts
Were sired....
.....
I tire of chasing the tail
Of my authenticity
In concentric and elliptical circles....
There is no ending,
Nor is there any valid reasoning.
It makes no sense.

Time ... Perhaps

Will the time ever come
When we cry no more,
Die no more,
Vie no more
For that which belongs to others

There is death on the streets,
In our homes,
In our schools,
And everywhere else
Man prevails

Perhaps,
Soon come the time
When words no longer matter,
For the 'hearers of the word'
Shall perish
And leave behind empty legacies,
For when we had the chance,
We did not
Love one and another

Perhaps,
Soon come the time
When most men
Will practice the evils
And avarice
Of hate, greed, bias,
And whatever other practices
That forge the instruments
Of a certain death
Of the soul of humanity

Perhaps,
We will awaken,
And collectively understand
That in order to survive
We must purge all the filth
That abides
Amongst us,
Around us
And within us,
Before there is no more
Us.

Perhaps 'Time'
Will be kind,
Or Perhaps
'Time' too
Will get tired
And run out of this house
Where iniquity grows
Without restraint

Who knows ....
In 'Time'
Perhaps ...
We will come to understand ...
Perhaps ... Perhaps.

February 2025 Featured Poets

~ * ~

Shafkat Aziz Hajam

Frosina Tasevska

Muhammad Gaddafi Masoud

Karen Morrison

i Fly

because

I Can

... said the Dreamer to the world.

www.iamjustbill.com

122

Shafkat
Aziz
Hajam

Shafkat Aziz Hajam

Shafkat Aziz Hajam is a India kashmir. He is a poet, reviewer and co-author. He is the author of one children poetry book titled as The cuckoo's voice and one adults poetry book titled as The Unknown Wounded Heart.

His poems have appeared in international magazines,anthologies and journals like Inner Child Press International USA, AZAHAR anthology Spain, SAARC anthology, Litlight literary magazine Pakistan, PLOTS CREATIVES online literary magazine USA,, Prodigy , digital literary magazine USA etc.

Her Love

I lost my beauty for the harsh time of my youth,

Yearned to rare it for my name after demise,

She didn't aid me to preserve my beauty.

She longed to preserve hers that would be mine too –

For this she did like me but alas ! my harsh time…..

I had to bear it alone ,

Her love was for my summer when fall reigned me .

The Lost Dream

The lost dream, I dreamt again ,

Couldn't fulfil it, oh ! it caused pain .

Its beauty was not altered a bit ,

Not even my desire for it .

I dreamt it again but untimely .

 I could only cry helplessly .

My cry and sigh it could hear,

Though it yearned , it wasn't fair

For it to be the dream of mine again

As like me , him it would cause pain

I Am Not Barren

I am not barren.

My fecundity has not dwindled yet ,

Enough as before to bringforth blossoms of all sorts and I

do .

Alas ! Frequent invasions of atrocious autumn

Debilitates their potency to bloom in full

To show my greatness in their daintiness and redolence

That would once captivate aves from overseas

To warble in praise of my nature.

O Heaven! Free me from this brutish autumn,

Can't endure it any more.

To glitter with my flair,

Let clement spring reign over me.

Frosina Tasevska

Frosina Taseuska

Frosina Tasevska, hailing from Shtip, Republic of Macedonia, is a versatile poet and writer proficient in English and Macedonian. With two solo poetry collections to her credit, Frosina's literary prowess extends across national and international platforms, including magazines, journals, and anthologies. Recognized with numerous awards, she seamlessly weaves her words into compelling narratives. Alongside her literary pursuits, Frosina serves as an educator, bringing her passion for language and creativity to the classroom.

Deep Thoughts

I am a dried springhead
among a meadow flower.
You are a playful stream
amidst desolated wastelands.
Could you please be a bright drop that flows?
Flow down my enclosed stones
and destroy all marginal impurities.
You are like a dark room
among an illuminated fireplace.
I am a luminous lantern
amidst a dark silence.
Let me be, at least a beam
to penetrate through the dark windows
and ruin the faceless apparitions!
I'm that kind of end without an ending
between two distances.
You are a bridge between two eternities.
Please be the clutch and connect those
two distances between two eternities!

I am a springhead without water.
You are water without a springhead.
You are that room without the light.
I am that light without the room.
I am a long distance without an ending.
You are a long ending in the distance.
The one that belongs to the other.
The one that cannot exist without the other.
So I wonder, why are we still alone?

My Horseman

In my thoughts, you never stop riding,
although without armor and a sword without a blade.
My eternal horseman!
The darkness is your turret of a staging battlefield
with all the distorted silhouettes of the time.
You whittled away
every sandstorm and thick snowdrift
always to protect me and preserve me,
so I could stay clean and unharmed.
And if I remember, and I remember well,
it has always been like this.

You were my horseman with a lion's heart,
I was your barefoot girl who looked just like you.
You're my constant blacksmith of a life's trickery,
I was your reflection on overgrowing.

Now, we are separated by two eternities,
two different worlds without a bridge to connect.
But you never stop riding in my thoughts
my eternal horseman, my beloved dad!

Don't Give Up, Don't Quit

If you're feeling down, shattered like an empty cup
No matter how complex your path is, *don't give up!*
Remember that anything worthwhile takes time
No wings to fly, but two feet to scale and climb.
When you feel like you're at the end of the rope
Don't ever underestimate your strength, and have hope.
People might try to talk you out of pursuing your goal
But only you can calm the insecurity inside your soul.

If you feel like you can't go on, don't you dare quit
Rest if you must, take a deep breath just a bit
For your breakthrough is just around the corner
And in all disorders, there is a secret order.

Life is not simple, it has its own twists and turns
but you must live and love the light that burns.
Never let your head hang down and grieve
but stand up proudly and fight for what you believe!

Muhammad Gaddafi Masoud

Muhammad Gaddafi Masoud

Muhammad Gaddafi Masoud obtained an intermediate diploma, specializing in theater arts, from the Jamal al-Din al-Miladi Institute in the Libyan capital, Tripoli, in 2000. He writes poetry in Arabic, and his poems have been published in various Arab newspapers and magazines. His collection of poetry was published in 2007 in Libya for a single edition. Some of his poems have also been translated into English, Spanish, Italian, Albanian, and Chinese, and published in newspapers, magazines, and websites in Italy, Argentina, Greece, China, Spain, Serbia, Romania, Bengal, and America.

A number of Arab critics wrote studies about his poetry and various critical readings published in well-known international newspapers and magazines, and his poems were among studies published in books and encyclopedias about poets in the world.

He extends his thanks to everyone who supported him by publishing and translating:

Professor Angela Costa. Albania
Dr. Abdul Hadi Saadoun. Iraq
Writer Suzan Ibrahim. Syria
Professor Nina Al-Sartawi. Libya
Ms. Raja Naqara. Tunisia

Cancer Sun

They agree at the end
They cry what falls out of the
nests .
They weave with tears the gardens of
Distant wishes .
And their hope is a luminous moon
Waiting for it with old gear
And laughter that broke
On a patience that has aged and remained his way.

Glorious.

The brown one sprouting in the grass
Frost rose.

Aisha.

The butterfly of colors in the pastures of the soul
A shadow of

After the disappointment

i watch it, it doesn't rain
i come taken, with what
i carry from certainty
then after the disappointment
except the dream.

Tale

on the verge of a tale
seagull fell, in
the water .

Messages

boiling the messages
the end invisibility
palm trees, are falling
in the valley of the flutes

Her gaze

were broken our lips on
the sight of her gaze .

lumberjack

gather firewood
bleeding sun
selled the horizon
at auction .

Happiness

lump from barking
the happiness

Muhammad Gaddafi Masoud

Division

divides the laughter itself
on itself
who closes the door of , a-ha

Translated by Neina Al-Sartawi

Childhood

Childhood
Immersed in the childhood of my mistakes,
Cannot distinguish an earthworm
From its mole.
I told the tree; my beloved
Then it bent to the wind

* *

I thought the bird was a bullet,
I threw myself on the ground,
When it flew away.

* *

I slept with the clock,
So orgasm arriving late,
At the Viagra time.

* *

I tried to hide behind my shoes,
But it betrayed me,
Moving aside.

* *

I walked crookedly,
Throwing shadows with a stone,
It bounced back as bullets and bleeding wane moons.

Translated into English by Suzan Ibrahim

Muhammad Gaddafi Masoud

Karen Morrison

Karen Morrison, an American Jamaican, is a singer/poet/writer and aspiring playwright. In 2007 Morrison began performing as a Reggae artist, opening for Maxi Priest, The Mighty Diamonds, and others. Dedicating her life to Christ in 2015, she rebranded herself as "Bryck Rose" and commenced working with Jamaican Gospel group, CREW 40:4. Her debut Gospel release titled Uoli Uoli Uoli (Holy, Holy, Holy), was a collaboration with Ethnodoxologist and Gospel Artiste, Jo-Ann Richards; she is currently producing her upcoming Gospel album, "Mountains". A reflective writer, Morrison proudly, published her anthology of poem, 'DEWDROPS: Heartical Poetry - English and Jamaican Patwa' (2021).

The Show

The rain came this afternoon
And played a song upon my zinc
A lullaby backed by the sweetest choral of Parakeets
Dressed in violet, amber, majestic blue and royal pink
Tapping out notes, unique and never to be heard again
Every rainfall, a new melody it sends
Rainforest green covered my bed
Drunk like a sailor, intoxicated with nature, I rested my head
I forsook my days duties to capture the time
Feeling blessed and Inspired, I wrote this precipitational rhyme
But before the ink could dry, the music stopped
I stood in the doorway to catch the final drops
The band had changed as the Robins began to sing
Out came, butterflies, earthworms and all kinds of creeping things
I truly thought the sun was jealous, the way He made his presence known
But I realized as He cast His rainbow
He, was the promoter of The Show

The Mighty Pen

At war with silence and solitude in this place
With my pen I take revenge, not a word will I erase
I scream upon the paper, I laugh at loneliness
What my mind could not contain
I released with strokes against the surface
I made it my servant, for the world to read
Paper was my playground
The ink had set me free
Permanent is the stain, going forth like a bow
If I am too careful, the truth you'll never know
Insult by ink, blunt trauma on paper
The tongue is very mighty but the pen it is no safer
By kings and ink prisoners have been loosed
From chains and bars authors are produced
Through sight and sound we deliver
Things we cannot retract
Ocular and audible emotions so exact
I write no lie, I write no fiction
I release my cogitation with precise mechanical diction
For once we could not read, we were not to be enlightened
But now I rule the alphabet, my enemies are frightened
Insult by ink, blunt trauma on paper
The tongue is very mighty
But the pen it is no safer

Seven

Seven days to sow, seven days to reap
I ain't got seven, only three minutes to speak
Lord I'm calling on you seven days a week
Hear my cry, humble and meek
Jericho walls fell on the seventh day
In my heart I'm marching, I know you hear my prayer
Psalm seven in thee I put my trust
Several things you love, but seven you hate so much
A proud look, a lying tongue, hands that shed innocent
blood
A heart that deviseth wicked imaginations, feet that be
swift, running to mischief
A false witness that speaketh lies, sowing discord among
the brethren
Lord hear my seventh cry
Sometimes I don't know what to do
But seven days of me, means seven days of you
Seven times rise from seven times fall
Lord you have no limit, you're not seven feet tall
You made the wonders of the world
More than seven I behold
So I give seven days of thanks, seven days of praise
You did it in three, it didn't take seven days

Remembering

our fallen soldiers of verse

Janet Perkins Caldwell
February 14, 1959 ~ September 20, 2016

Alan W. Jankowski
16 March 1961 ~ 10 March 2017

The Butterfly Effect

"15" in effect

Inner Child Press
News

Published Books

by

Poetry Posse Members

We are so excited to share and announce a few of the current books, as well as the new and upcoming books of some of our Poetry Posse authors.

On the following pages we present to you ...

Alicja Maria Kuberska

Jackie Davis Allen

Gail Weston Shazor

hülya n. yılmaz

Nizar Sartawi

Elizabeth E. Castillo

Faleeha Hassan

Fahredin Shehu

Kimberly Burnham

Caroline 'Ceri' Nazareno

Eliza Segiet

Teresa E. Gallion

Mutawaf Shaheed

William S. Peters, Sr.

Now Available

www.innerchildpress.com

KREW ŻYCIA

The Blood of Life

Eliza Segiet

Translated by Dorota Stępińska

Now Available

www.innerchildpress.com

An Ode to Love

Love Prevails

William S. Peters, Sr.

Now Available

www.innerchildpress.com

Bir Zamanlar

Türkiye'de

hülya n. yılmaz

Now Available
www.innerchildpress.com

I Am in Your Head

C. E. Shy

Now Available

www.innerchildpress.com

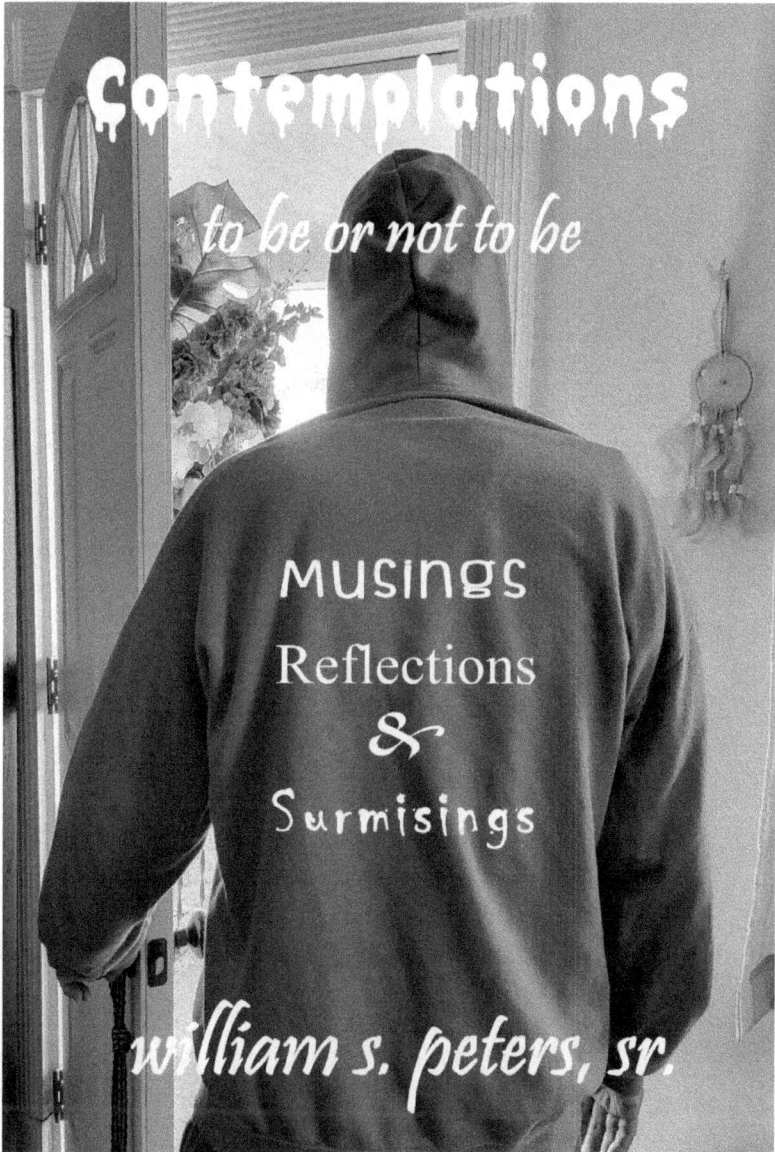

Contemplations

to be or not to be

musings

Reflections

&

Surmisings

william s. peters, sr.

Now Available

www.innerchildpress.com

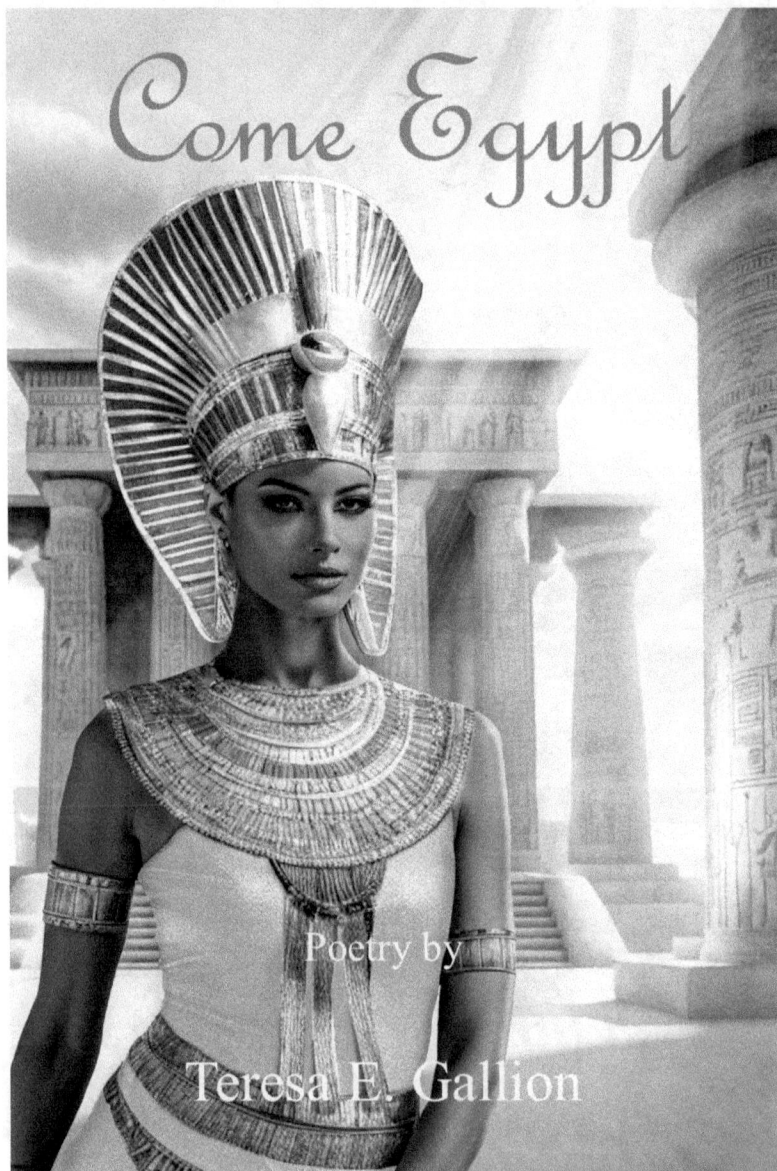

Come Egypt

Poetry by

Teresa E. Gallion

Now Available

www.innerchildpress.com

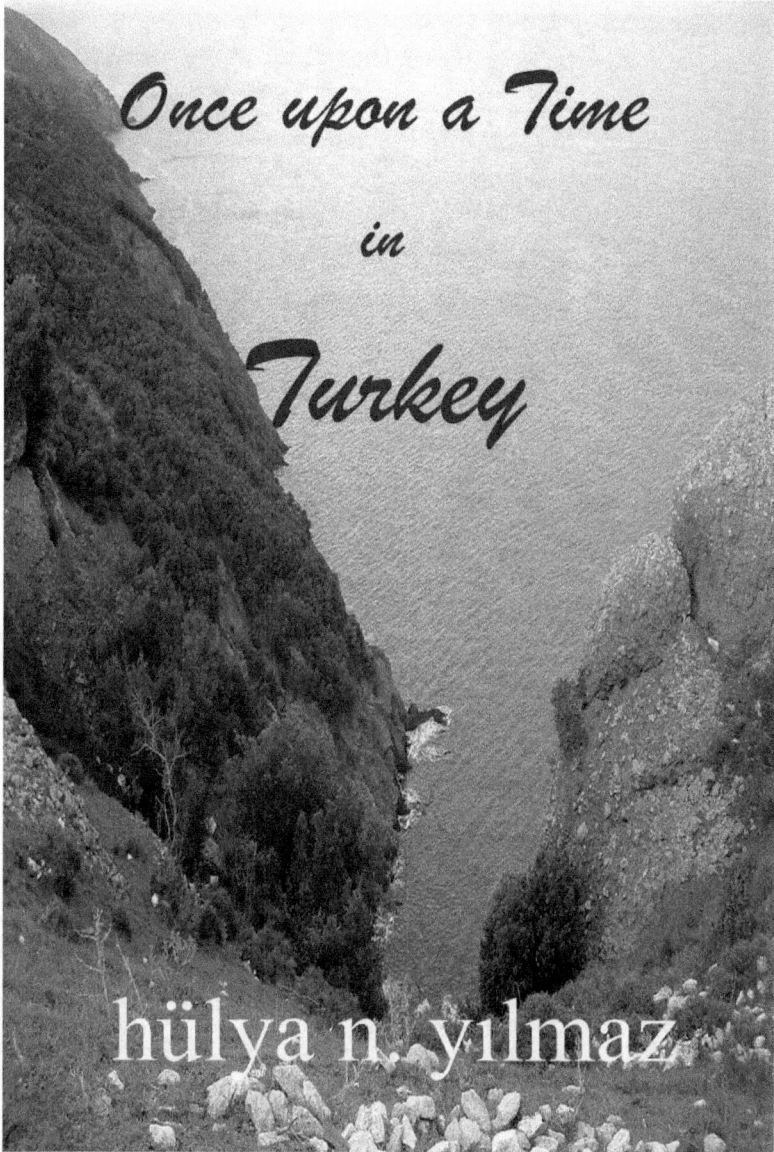

Once upon a Time
in
Turkey

hülya n. yılmaz

Now Available
www.innerchildpress.com

159

Unapologetically

BLACK

&

Blues

william s. peters, sr.

Now Available

www.innerchildpress.com

Pulling Coats

Shareef Abdur-Rasheed

Now Available
www.innerchildpress.com

UMAMI
The Essence of Deliciousness

Fahredin Shehu

Now Available
www.innerchildpress.com

After the Frost

Alicja Maria Kuberska

Now Available

www.innerchildpress.com

Fahredin Shehu

ORMUS

Now Available

www.innerchildpress.com

Ahead of My Time

. . . from the Streets to the Stages

Albert 'Infinite' Carrasco

Now Available
www.innerchildpress.com

Eliza Segiet

To Be More

Now Available at
www.innerchildpress.com

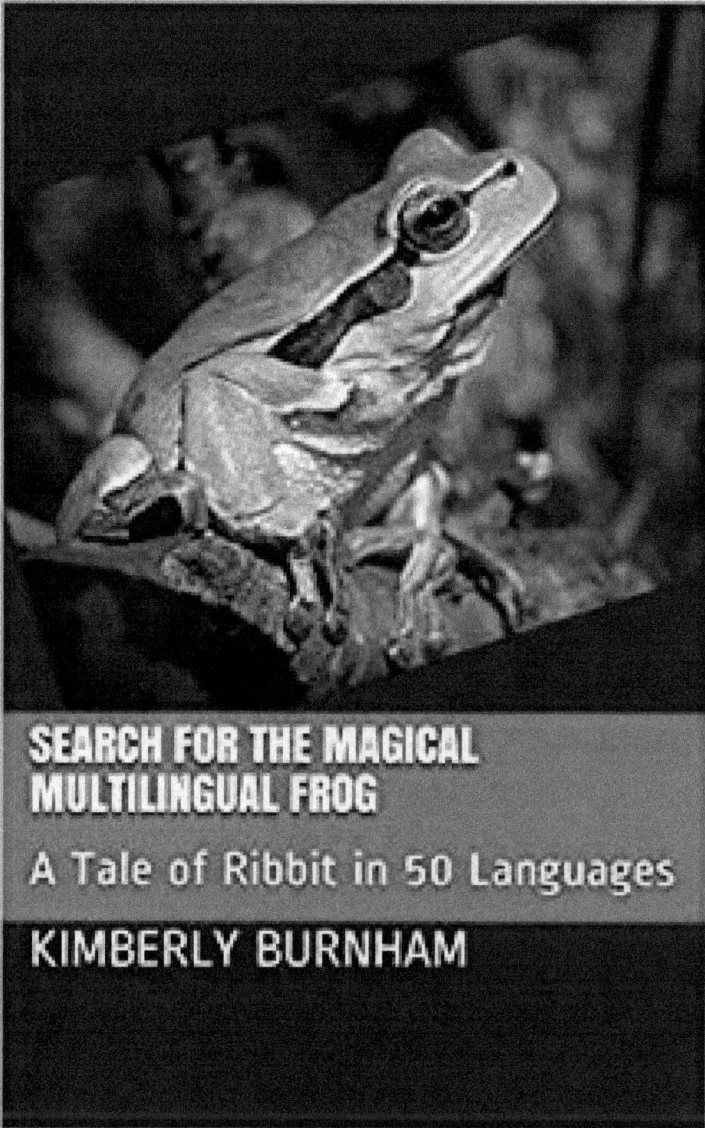

SEARCH FOR THE MAGICAL
MULTILINGUAL FROG

A Tale of Ribbit in 50 Languages

KIMBERLY BURNHAM

Now Available at

www.amazon.com/gp/product/B08MYL5B7S/ref=
dbs_a_def_rwt_hsch_vapi_tkin_p1_i2

167

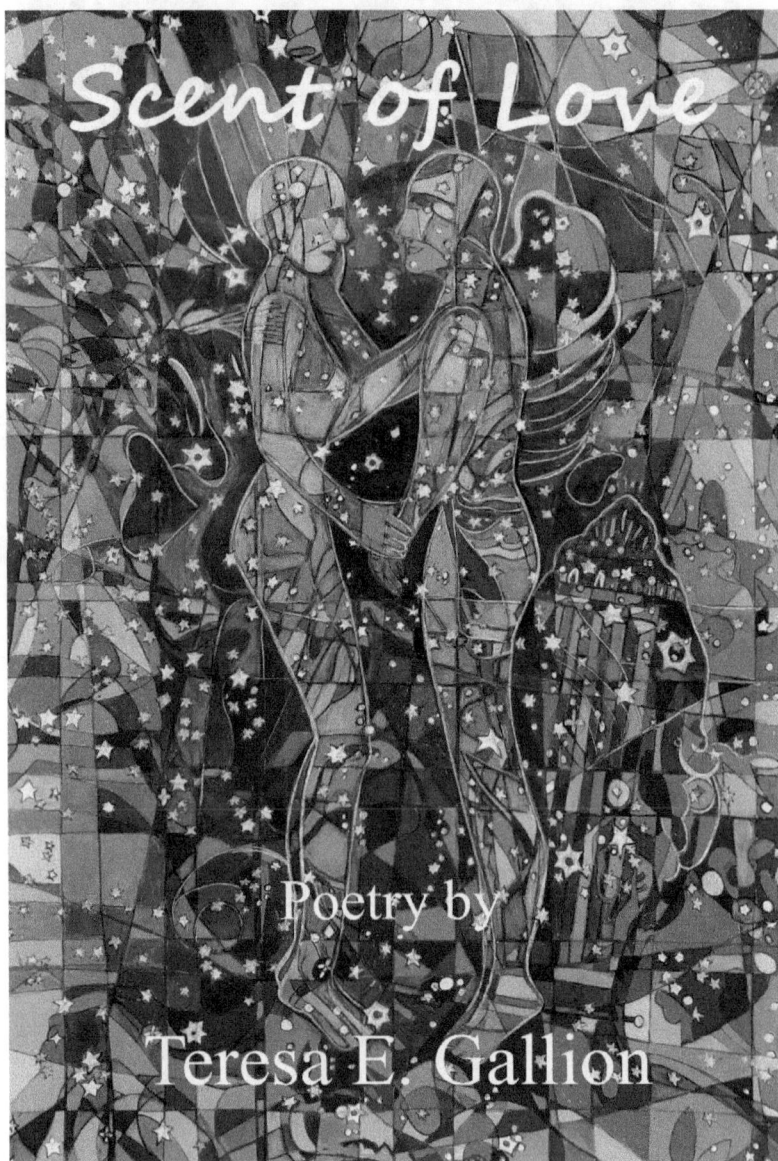

Scent of Love

Poetry by

Teresa E. Gallion

Now Available
www.innerchildpress.com

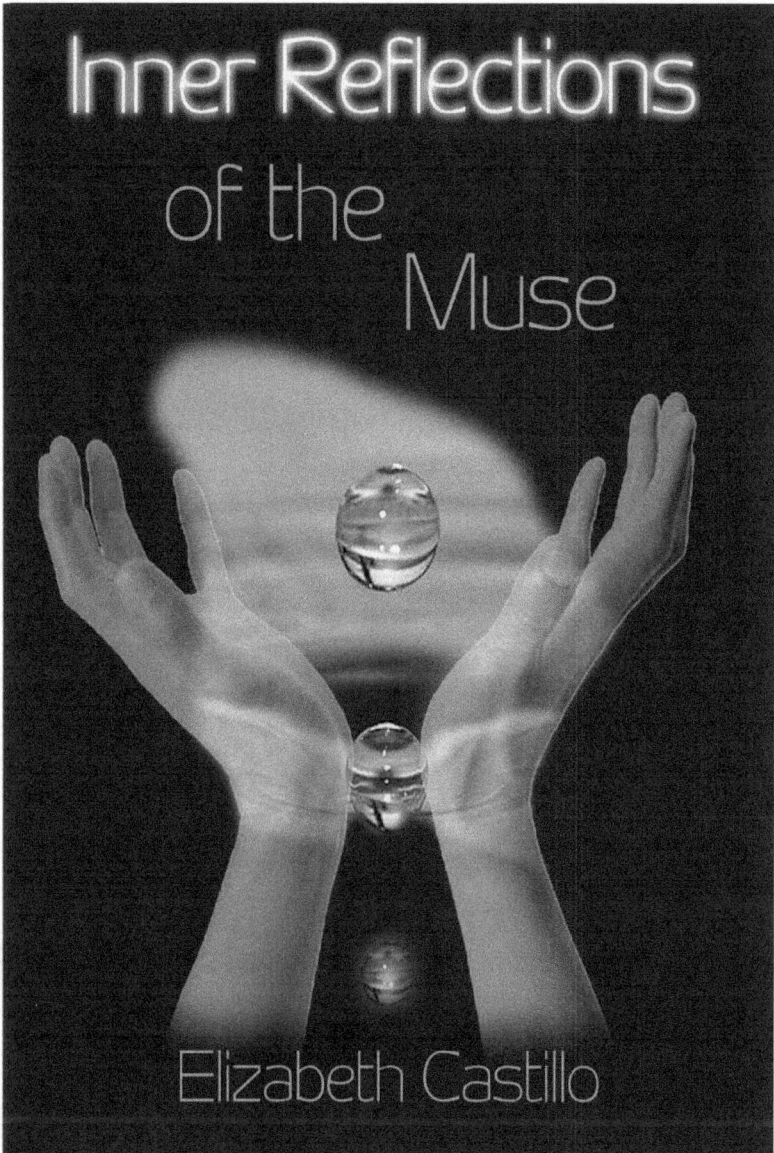

Inner Reflections
of the
Muse

Elizabeth Castillo

Now Available
www.innerchildpress.com

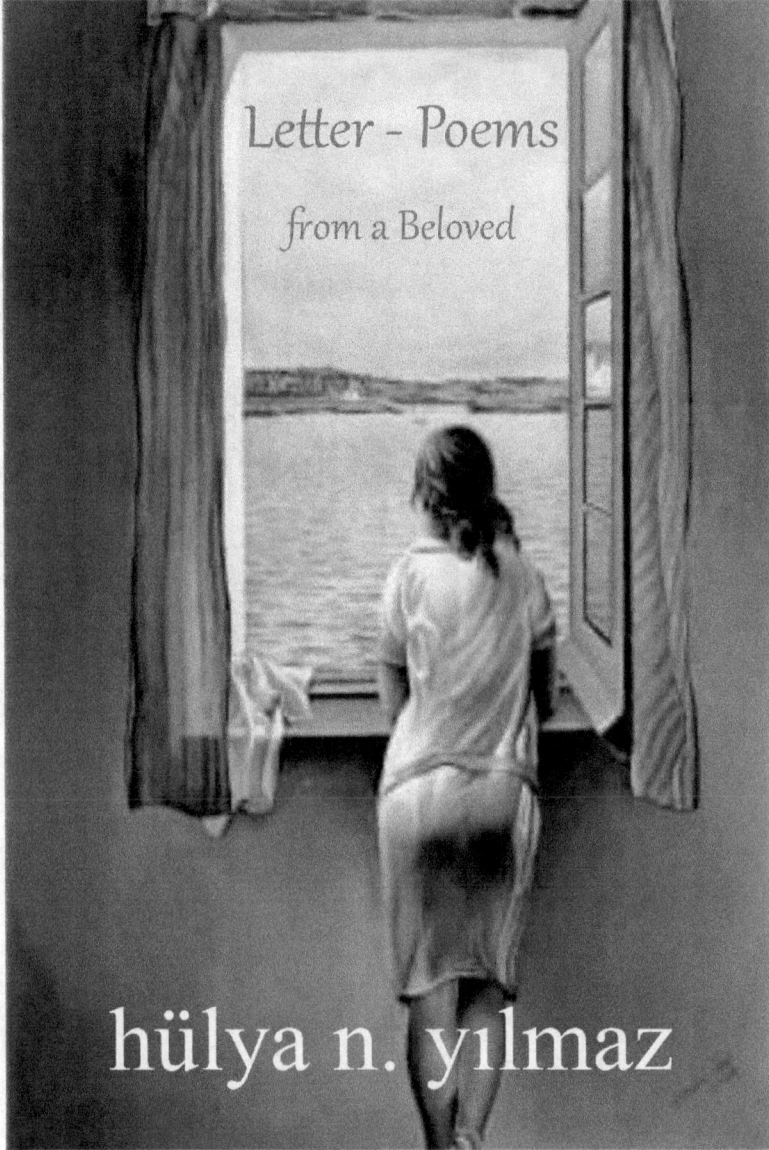

Letter - Poems

from a Beloved

hülya n. yılmaz

Now Available

www.innerchildpress.com

Now Available

www.innerchildpress.com

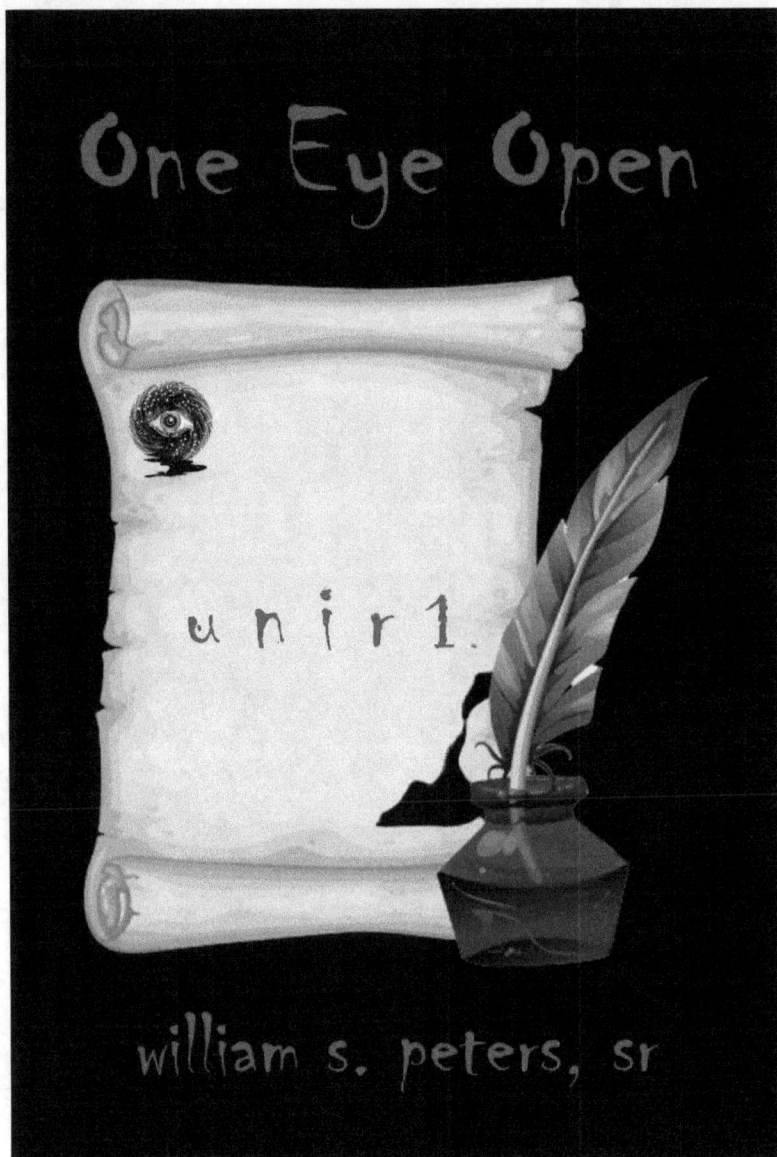

One Eye Open

u n i r 1.

william s. peters, sr

Now Available
www.innerchildpress.com

The Book of krisar

volume v

william s. peters, sr.

Now Available

www.innerchildpress.com

The Book of krisar

Volume I

william s. peters, sr.

The Book of krisar

Volume II

william s. peters, sr.

Now Available

www.innerchildpress.com

The Book of krisar

Volume III

william s. peters, sr.

The Book of krisar

Volume IV

william s. peters, sr.

Now Available

www.innerchildpress.com

*V*elvet *P*assions

of

Calibrated Quarks

Caroline Nazareno-Gabis

Now Available

www.innerchildpress.com

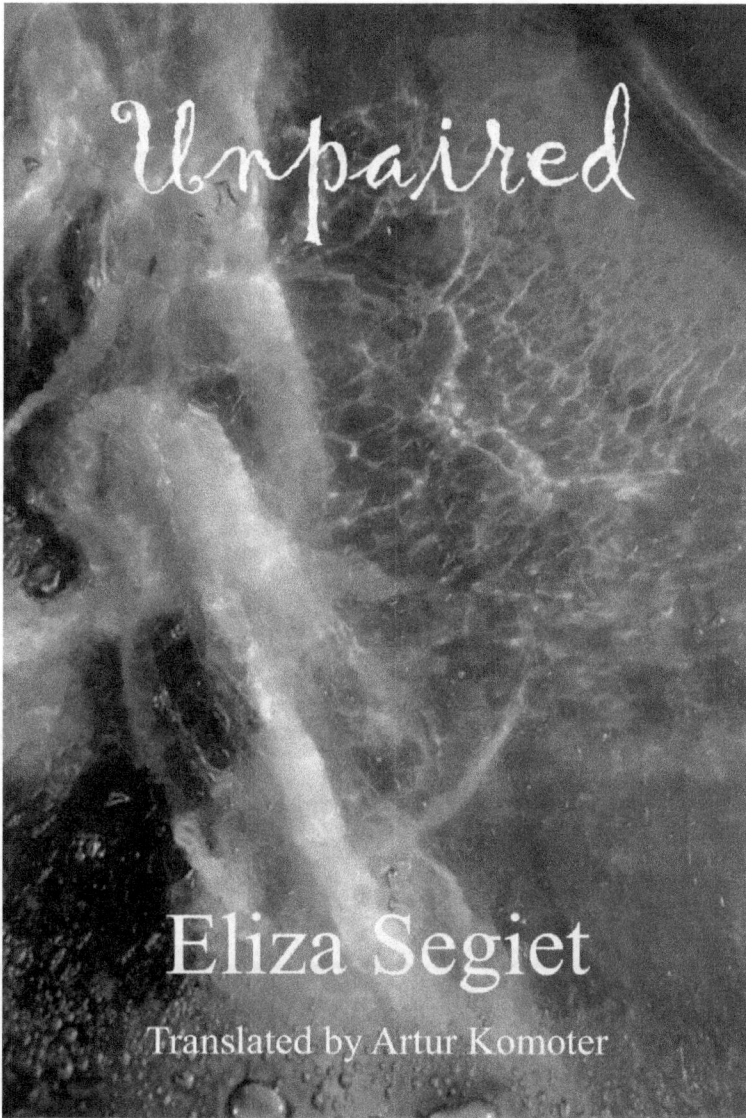

Unpaired

Eliza Segiet

Translated by Artur Komoter

Private Issue
www.innerchildpress.com

Canlarım

My Lifeblood

poetry in Turkish and English

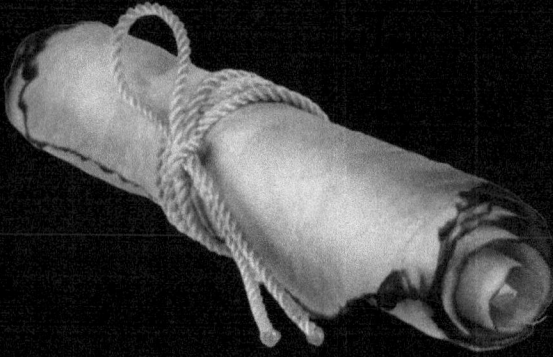

hülya n. yılmaz

Now Available

www.innerchildpress.com

Butterfly's Voice

Faleeha Hassan

Translated by William M. Hutchins

Now Available at
www.innerchildpress.com

No Illusions

Through the Looking Glass

Jackie Davis Allen

Now Available at
www.innerchildpress.com

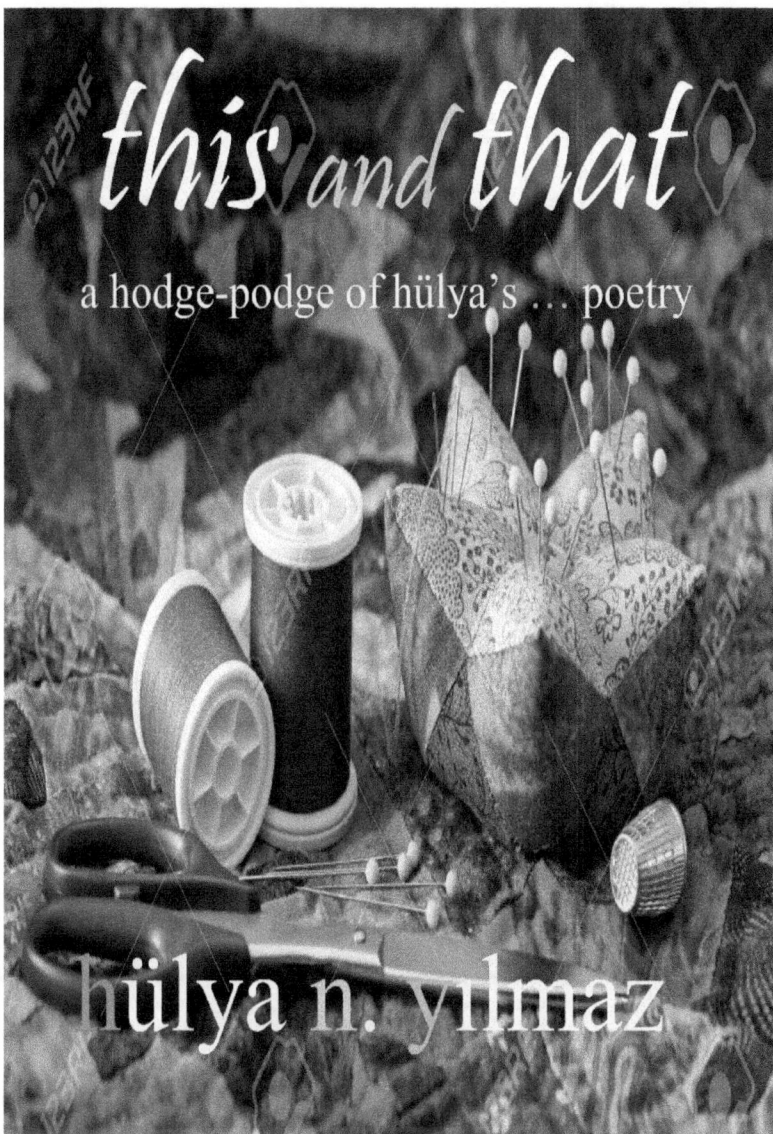

this and that

a hodge-podge of hülya's ... poetry

hülya n. yılmaz

Now Available at

www.innerchildpress.com

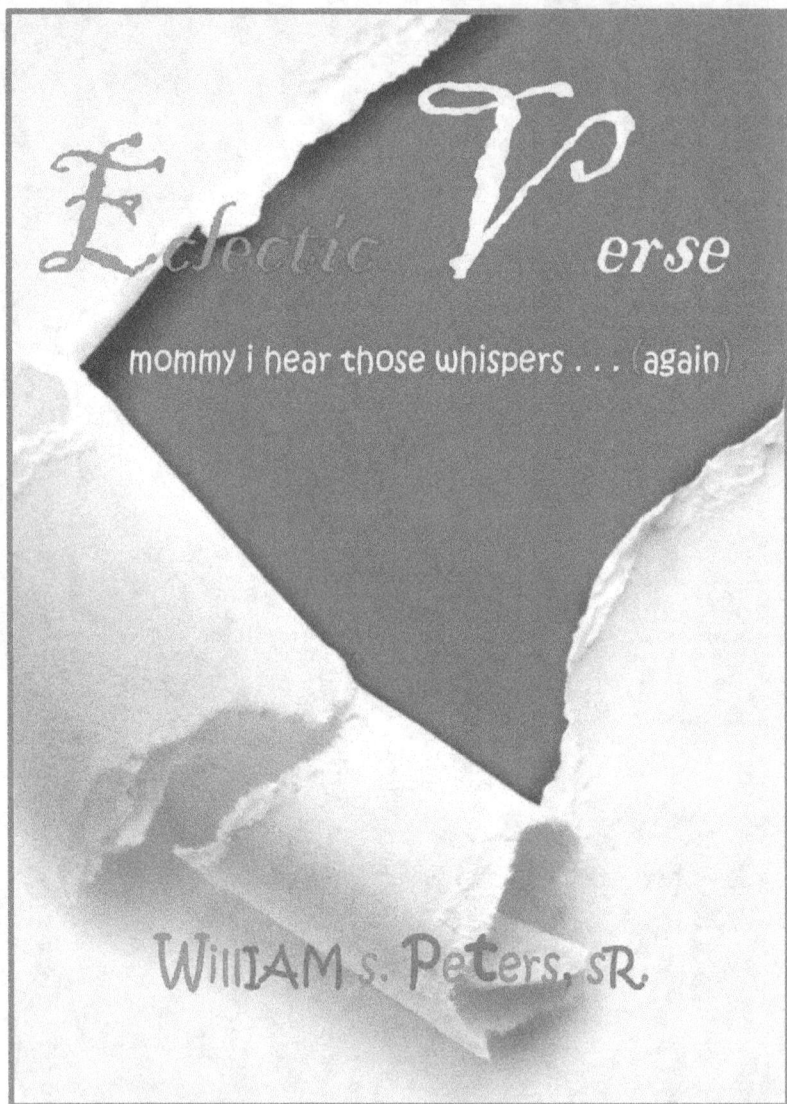

Eclectic Verse

mommy i hear those whispers . . . (again)

WilliAM s. PeTers, sR.

Now Available at
www.innerchildpress.com

HERENOW

FAHREDIN SHEHU

Magnetic People

Eliza Segiet

Translated by Artur Komoter

Now Available at

www.innerchildpress.com

Dark Side

of the

Moon

Jackie Davis Allen

Now Available at

www.innerchildpress.com

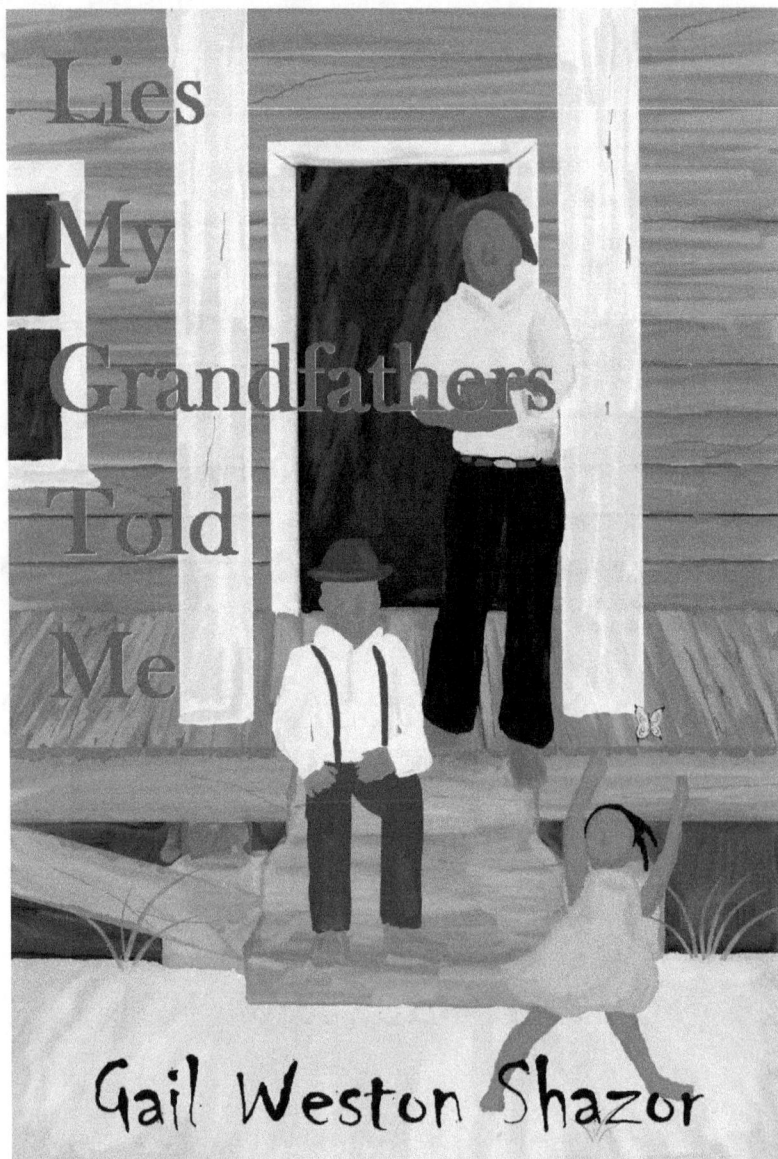

Lies
My
Grandfathers
Told
Me

Gail Weston Shazor

Now Available at
www.innerchildpress.com

Aflame

Memoirs in Verse

hülya n. yılmaz

Now Available at
www.innerchildpress.com

Mass Graves

Faleeha Hassan

Now Available at
www.innerchildpress.com

Breakfast

for

Butterflies

Faleeha Hassan

Now Available at
www.innerchildpress.com

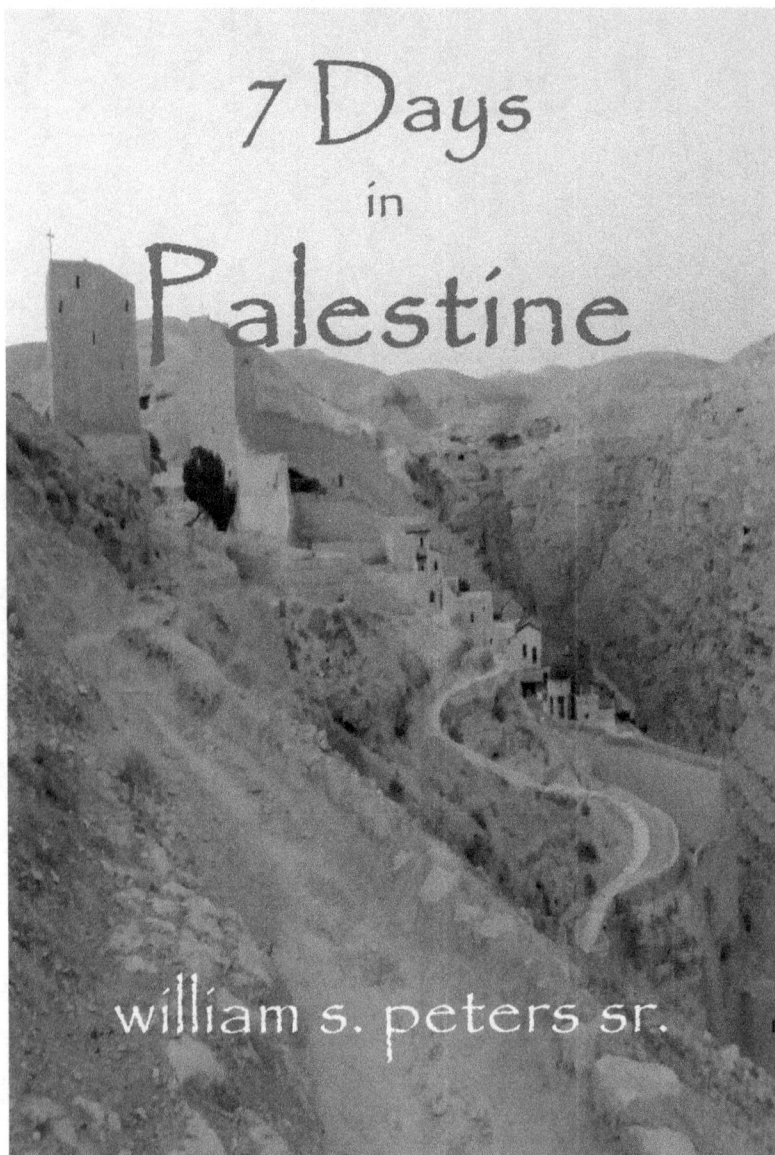

7 Days
in
Palestine

william s. peters sr.

Now Available at

www.innerchildpress.com

inner child press

presents

Tunisian Dreams

william s. peters, sr.

Now Available at

www.innerchildpress.com

Think on These Things
Book II

william s. peters, sr.

Now Available at
www.innerchildpress.com

my inner garden

~ expressions and discoveries ~

by

William S. Peters, Sr.

Now Available

www.innerchildpress.com

Other
Anthological
works from

Inner Child Press International

www.innerchildpress.com

Now Available

www.worldhealingworldpeacepoetry.com

Now Available
www.worldhealingworldpeacepoetry.com

World Healing
World Peace
2022

Poets for Humanity

Now Available

www.worldhealingworldpeacepoetry.com

World Healing World Peace
2020

Poets for Humanity

Now Available

www.worldhealingworldpeacepoetry.com

I WANT TO

LIVE

an examination of Black & White issues

POETRY

ANALYSES

STORIES

CREATIVE WRITING

CRITICAL ESSAYS

WRITERS FOR HUMANITY

Now Available

www.innerchildpress.com

Inner Child Press International
&
The Year of the Poet
present

Poetry

the best of 2020

Poets of the World

Now Available

www.innerchildpress.com

Inner Child Press International

presents

W.A.R.

We Are Revolution

Poets for Humanity

Now Available

www.innerchildpress.com

the Heart of a Poet

words for a better tomorrow

The Conscious Poets

Now Available

www.innerchildpress.com

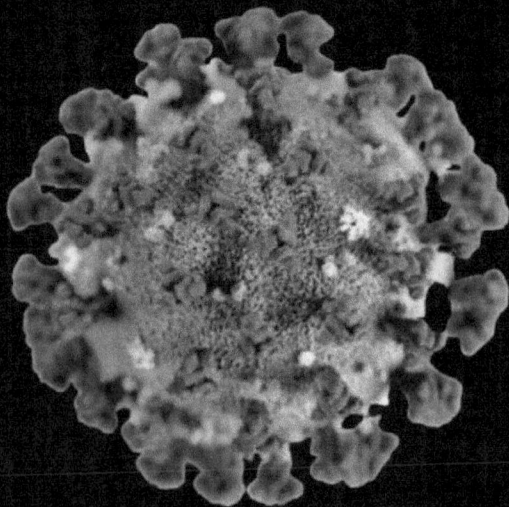

Corona

Social Distancing

Poets for Humanity

Now Available

www.innerchildpress.com

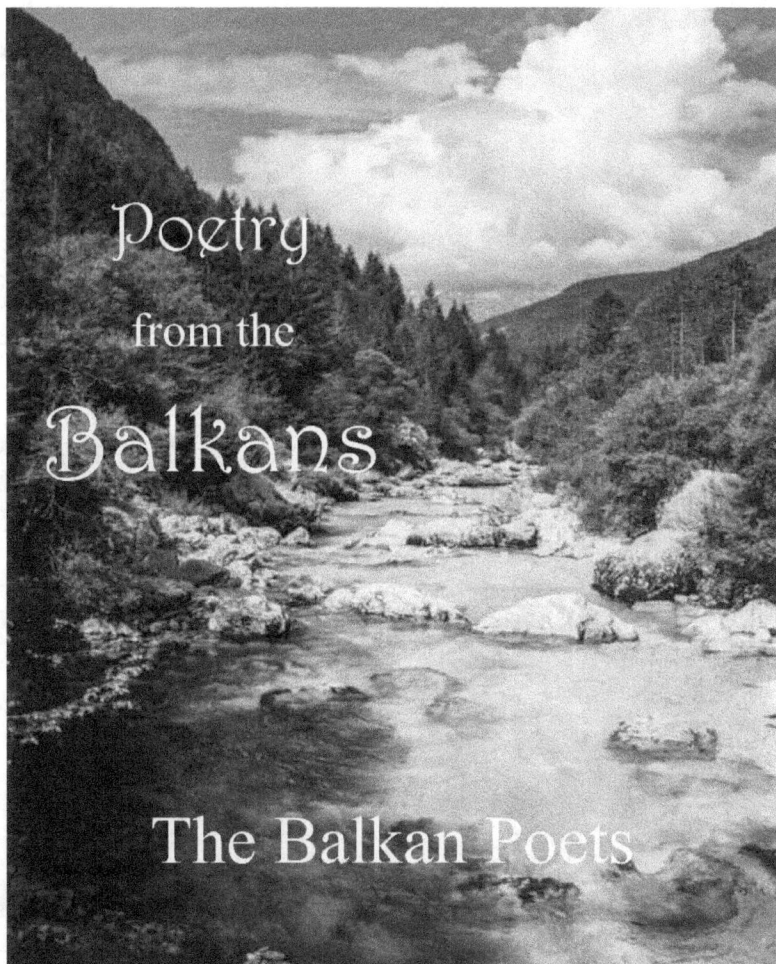

Poetry
from the
Balkans

The Balkan Poets

Now Available at
www.innerchildpress.com

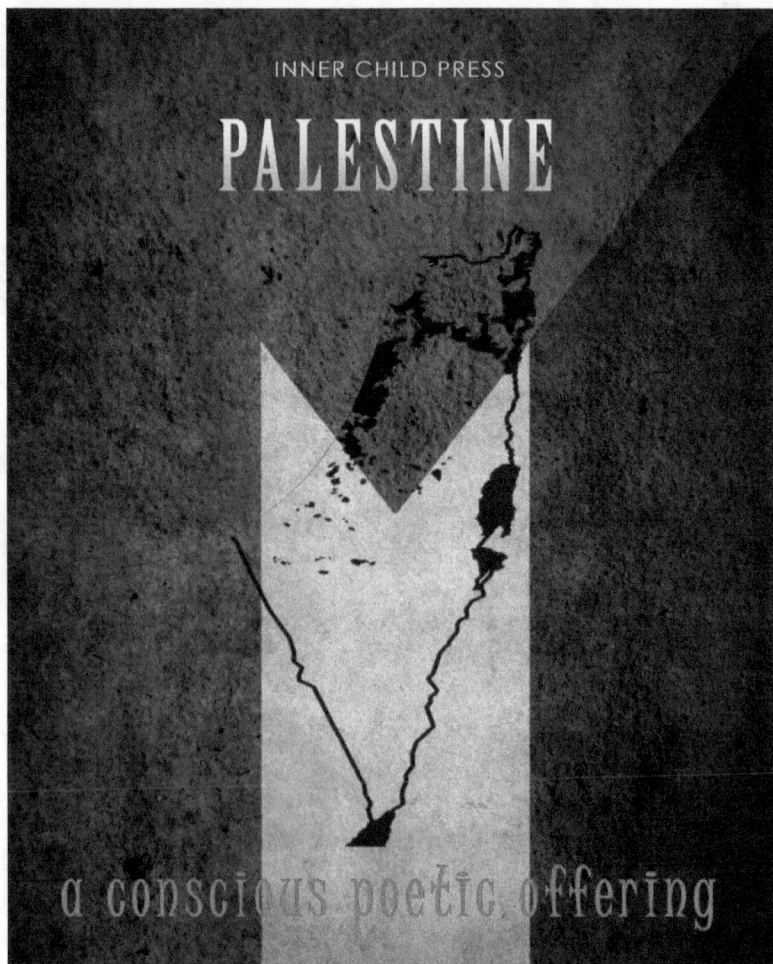

INNER CHILD PRESS

PALESTINE

a conscious poetic offering

Now Available at
www.innerchildpress.com

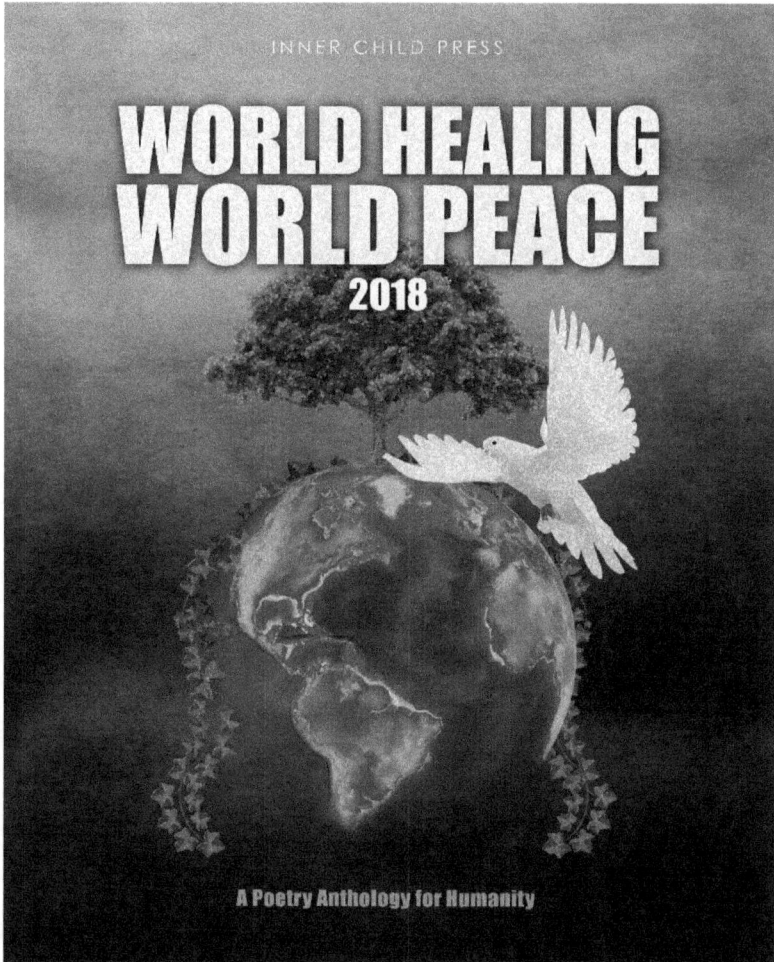

Now Available at
www.innerchildpress.com

Inner Child Press International
presents

A Love Anthology

2019

The Love Poets

Now Available

www.worldhealingworldpeacepoetry.com

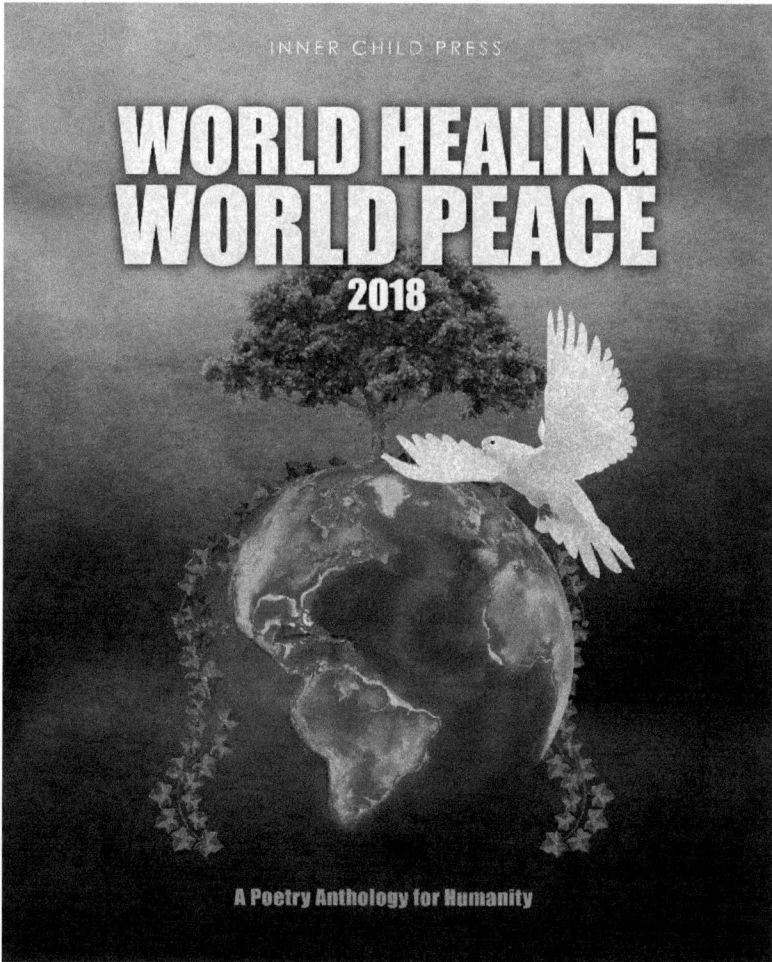

INNER CHILD PRESS

WORLD HEALING WORLD PEACE
2018

A Poetry Anthology for Humanity

Now Available

www.worldhealingworldpeacepoetry.com

Now Available

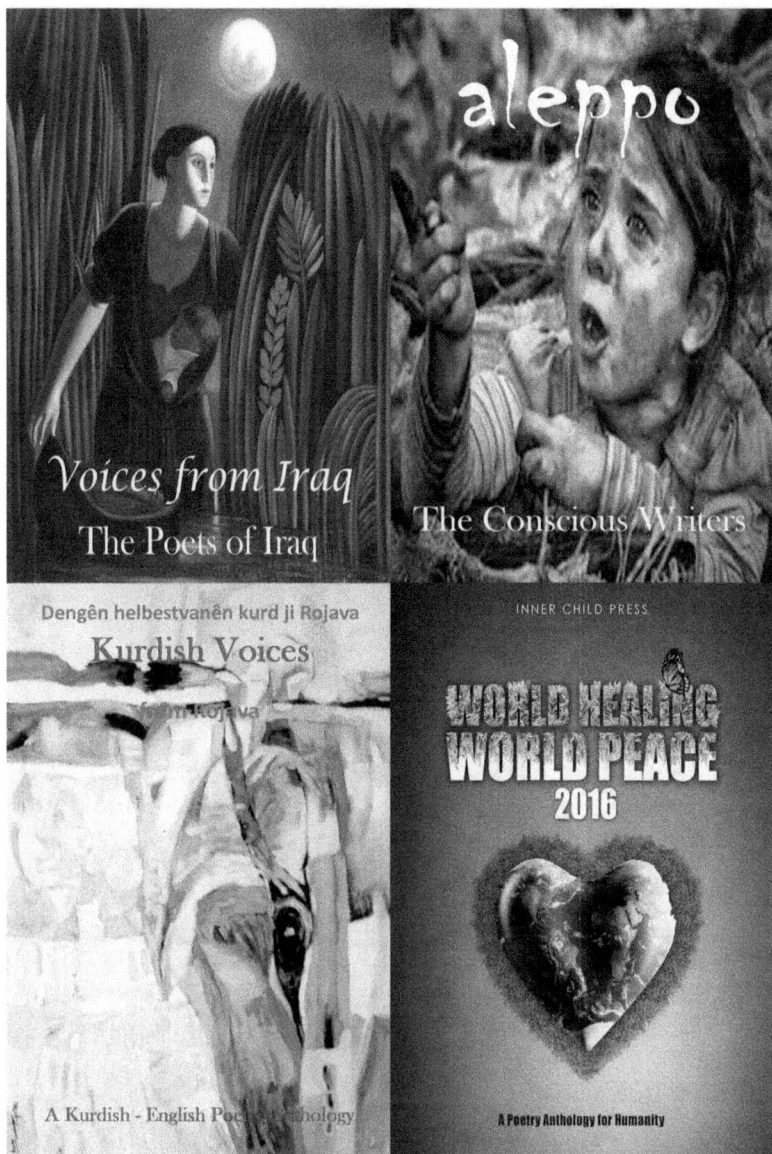

Now Available

www.innerchildpress.com/anthologies

healing through words

Poetry ... Prose ... Prayer ... Stories

Janet

gone too soon . . .

a
Poetically
Spoken
Anthology
volume I
Collector's Edition

The Poetry Posse
Presents

an anthology
of

Love

The Poetry Posse 2016

i want my POETRY to . . .

a collection of the Voices of Many inspired by . . .

Monte Smith

i want my POETRY to . . .

a collection of the Voices of Many inspired by . . .

Monte Smith

volume II

i want my POETRY to . . . volume 3

a collection of the Voices of Many inspired by . . .

Monte Smith

11 Words

(9 lines . . .)

for those who are challenged

an anthology of Poetry inspired by . . .

Poetry Dancer

Now Available

www.innerchildpress.com/anthologies

The Year of the Poet
January 2014

The Poetry Posse

Jamie Bond
Gail Weston Shazor
Albert 'Infinite' Carrasco
Siddartha Beth Pierce
Janet P. Caldwell
June 'Bugg' Barefield
Debbie M. Allen
Tony Henninger
Joe DaVerbal Minddancer
Robert Gibbons
Neetu Wali
Shareef Abdur-Rasheed
William S. Peters, Sr.

Carnation

Our January Feature
Terri L. Johnson

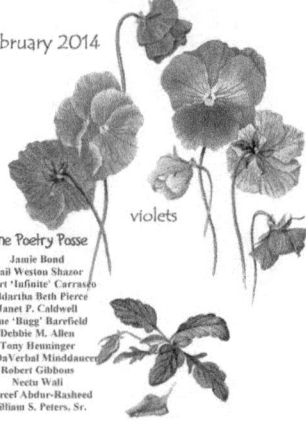

the Year of the Poet
February 2014

violets

The Poetry Posse

Jamie Bond
Gail Weston Shazor
Albert 'Infinite' Carrasco
Siddartha Beth Pierce
Janet P. Caldwell
June 'Bugg' Barefield
Debbie M. Allen
Tony Henninger
Joe DaVerbal Minddancer
Robert Gibbons
Neetu Wali
Shareef Abdur-Rasheed
William S. Peters, Sr.

Our February Features
Teresa E. Gallion & Robert Gibson

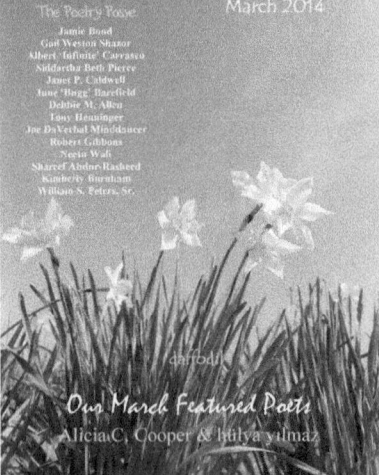

the Year of the Poet
March 2014

The Poetry Posse

Jamie Bond
Gail Weston Shazor
Albert 'Infinite' Carrasco
Siddartha Beth Pierce
Janet P. Caldwell
June 'Bugg' Barefield
Debbie M. Allen
Tony Henninger
Joe DaVerbal Minddancer
Robert Gibbons
Neetu Wali
Shareef Abdur-Rasheed
Kimberly Burnham
William S. Peters, Sr.

daffodil

Our March Featured Poets
Alicia C. Cooper & hülya yılmaz

the Year of the Poet
April 2014

The Poetry Posse

Jamie Bond
Gail Weston Shazor
Albert 'Infinite' Carrasco
Siddartha Beth Pierce
Janet P. Caldwell
June 'Bugg' Barefield
Debbie M. Allen
Tony Henninger
Joe DaVerbal Minddancer
Robert Gibbons
Neetu Wali
Shareef Abdur-Rasheed
Kimberly Burnham
William S. Peters, Sr.

Our April Featured Poets
Fahredin Shehu
Martina Reisz Newberry
Justin Blackburn
Monte Smith

Sweet Pea

celebrating international poetry month

Now Available
www.innerchildpress.com/the-year-of-the-poet

the year of the poet
May 2014

May's Featured Poets

ReeCee
Joski the Poet
Shannon Stanton

Dedicated to our Children

The Poetry Posse

Jamie Bond
Gail Weston Shazor
Albert 'Infinite' Carrasco
Siddartha Beth Pierce
Janet P. Caldwell
Jackie 'Bugg' Barefield
Debbie M. Allen
Tony Henninger
Joe DeVerbal Minddancer
Robert Gibbons
Neetu Wali
Shareef Abdur-Rasheed
Kimberly Burnham
William S. Peters, Sr.

Lily of the Valley

the Year of the Poet
June 2014

Love & Relationship

Rose

June's Featured Poets
Shantelle McLin
Jacqueline D. E. Kennedy
Abraham N. Benjamin

The Poetry Posse
Jamie Bond
Gail Weston Shazor
Albert 'Infinite' Carrasco
Siddartha Beth Pierce
Janet P. Caldwell
June 'Bugg' Barefield
Debbie M. Allen
Tony Henninger
Joe DeVerbal Minddancer
Robert Gibbons
Neetu Wali
Shareef Abdur-Rasheed
Kimberly Burnham
William S. Peters, Sr.

The Year of the Poet
July 2014

July Feature Poets

Christena A.V. Williams
Pri-John R. Strum
Kolade Olanrewaju Freedom

The Poetry Posse
Jamie Bond
Gail Weston Shazor
Albert 'Infinite' Carrasco
Siddartha Beth Pierce
Janet P. Caldwell
June 'Bugg' Barefield
Debbie M. Allen
Tony Henninger
Joe DeVerbal Minddancer
Robert Gibbons
Neetu Wali
Shareef Abdur-Rasheed
Kimberly Burnham
William S. Peters, Sr.

Lotus
Asian Flower of the Month

The Year of the Poet
August 2014

Gladiolus

The Poetry Posse
Jamie Bond
Gail Weston Shazor
Albert 'Infinite' Carrasco
Siddartha Beth Pierce
Janet P. Caldwell
June 'Bugg' Barefield
Debbie M. Allen
Tony Henninger
Joe DeVerbal Minddancer
Robert Gibbons
Neetu Wali
Shareef Abdur-Rasheed
Kimberly Burnham
William S. Peters, Sr.

August Feature Poets

Ann White * Rosalind Cherry * Sheila Jenkins

Now Available

www.innerchildpress.com/the-year-of-the-poet

The Year of the Poet
September 2014
Aster   Morning-Glory
Wild Chestnut September Birth Flower
September Feature Poets
Florence Malone * Keith Alan Hamilton

The Poetry Posse
Jamie Bond * Gail Weston Shazor * Albert 'Infinite' Carrasco * Siddartha Beth Pierce
Janet P. Caldwell * June 'Bugg' Barefield * Debbie M. Allen * Tony Henninger
Joe DaVerbal Minddancer * Robert Gibbons * Neetu Wali * Shareef Abdur-Rasheed
Kimberly Burnham * William S. Peters, Sr.

THE YEAR OF THE POET
October 2014
Red Poppy

The Poetry Posse
Jamie Bond * Gail Weston Shazor * Albert 'Infinite' Carrasco * Siddartha Beth Pierce
Janet P. Caldwell * June 'Bugg' Barefield * Debbie M. Allen * Tony Henninger
Joe DaVerbal Minddancer * Robert Gibbons * Neetu Wali * Shareef Abdur-Rasheed
Kimberly Burnham * William S. Peters, Sr.

October Feature Poets
Ceri Naz * Rajendra Padhi * Elizabeth Castillo

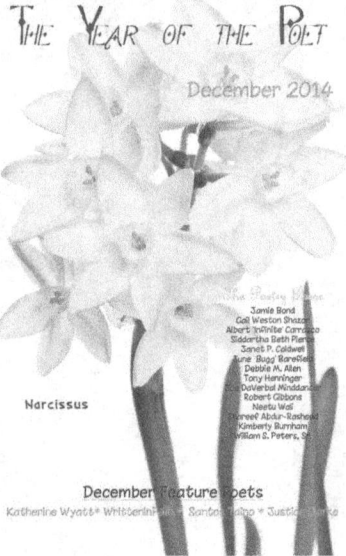

THE YEAR OF THE POET
November 2014
Chrysanthemum

The Poetry Posse
Jamie Bond * Gail Weston Shazor * Albert 'Infinite' Carrasco * Siddartha Beth Pierce
Janet P. Caldwell * June 'Bugg' Barefield * Debbie M. Allen * Tony Henninger
Joe DaVerbal Minddancer * Robert Gibbons * Neetu Wali * Shareef Abdur-Rasheed
Kimberly Burnham * William S. Peters, Sr.

November Feature Poets
Jocelyn Mosman * Jackie Allen * James Moore * Neville Hiatt

THE YEAR OF THE POET
December 2014
Narcissus

The Poetry Posse
Jamie Bond
Gail Weston Shazor
Albert 'Infinite' Carrasco
Siddartha Beth Pierce
Janet P. Caldwell
June 'Bugg' Barefield
Debbie M. Allen
Tony Henninger
Joe DaVerbal Minddancer
Robert Gibbons
Neetu Wali
Shareef Abdur-Rasheed
Kimberly Burnham
William S. Peters, Sr.

December Feature Poets
Katherine Wyatt * WhitterinPoet * Santa Indigo * Justin Banks

Now Available

www.innerchildpress.com/the-year-of-the-poet

THE YEAR OF THE POET II
January 2015

Garnet

The Poetry Posse
Jamie Bond
Gail Weston Shazor
Albert 'Infinite' Carrasco
Siddartha Beth Pierce
Janet P. Caldwell
Tony Henninger
Joe DaVerbal Minddancer
Robert Gibbons
Neetu Wali
Shareef Abdur – Rasheed
Kimberly Burnham
Ann White
Keith Alan Hamilton
Katherine Wyatt
Fahredin Shehu
Hülya N. Yılmaz
Teresa E. Gallion
Jackie Allen
William S. Peters, Sr.

January Feature Poets
Bismay Mohanti * Jen Walls * Eric Judah

THE YEAR OF THE POET II
February 2015

Amethyst

THE POETRY POSSE
Jamie Bond
Gail Weston Shazor
Albert 'Infinite' Carrasco
Siddartha Beth Pierce
Janet P. Caldwell
Tony Henninger
Joe DaVerbal Minddancer
Robert Gibbons
Neetu Wali
Shareef Abdur – Rasheed
Kimberly Burnham
Ann White
Keith Alan Hamilton
Katherine Wyatt
Yılmaz
E. Gallion
Jackie Allen
William S. Peters, Sr.

FEBRUARY FEATURE POETS
Iram Fatima * Bob McNeil * Kerstin Centervall

The Year of the Poet II
March 2015

Our Featured Poets
Heung Sook * Anthony Arnold * Alicia Poland

Bloodstone

The Poetry Posse 2015
Jamie Bond * Gail Weston Shazor * Albert 'Infinite' Carrasco
Siddartha Beth Pierce * Janet P. Caldwell * Tony Henninger
Joe DaVerbal Minddancer * Neetu Wali * Shareef Abdur – Rasheed
Kimberly Burnham * Ann White * Keith Alan Hamilton
Katherine Wyatt * Fahredin Shehu * Hülya N. Yılmaz
Teresa E. Gallion * Jackie Allen * William S. Peters. Sr

The Year of the Poet II
April 2015

Celebrating International Poetry Month

Our Featured Poets
Raja Williams * Dennis Ferado * Laure Charazac

Diamonds

The Poetry Posse 2015
Jamie Bond * Gail Weston Shazor * Albert 'Infinite' Carrasco
Siddartha Beth Pierce * Janet P. Caldwell * Tony Henninger
Joe DaVerbal Minddancer * Neetu Wali * Shareef Abdur – Rasheed
Kimberly Burnham * Ann White * Keith Alan Hamilton
Katherine Wyatt * Fahredin Shehu * Hülya N. Yılmaz
Teresa E. Gallion * Jackie Allen * William S. Peters. Sr

Now Available

www.innerchildpress.com/the-year-of-the-poet

The Year of the Poet II
May 2015

May's Featured Poets
Geri Algeri
Akin Mosi Chinnery
Anna Jakubcza

Emeralds

The Poetry Posse 2015
Jamie Bond * Gail Weston Shazor * Albert 'Infinite' Carrasco
Siddartha Beth Pierce * Janet P. Caldwell * Tony Henninger
Joe DaVerbal Minddancer * Neetu Wali * Shareef Abdur – Rasheed
Kimberly Burnham * Ann White * Keith Alan Hamilton
Katherine Wyatt * Fahredin Shehu * Hülya N. Yılmaz
Teresa E. Gallion * Jackie Allen * William S. Peters, Sr.

The Year of the Poet II
June 2015

June's Featured Poets
Anahit Arustamyan * Yvette D. Murrell * Regina A. Walker

Pearl

The Poetry Posse 2015
Jamie Bond * Gail Weston Shazor * Albert 'Infinite' Carrasco
Siddartha Beth Pierce * Janet P. Caldwell * Tony Henninger
Joe DaVerbal Minddancer * Neetu Wali * Shareef Abdur – Rasheed
Kimberly Burnham * Ann White * Keith Alan Hamilton
Katherine Wyatt * Fahredin Shehu * Hülya N. Yılmaz
Teresa E. Gallion * Jackie Allen * William S. Peters, Sr.

The Year of the Poet II
July 2015

The Featured Poets for July 2015
Abhik Shome * Christina Neal * Robert Neal

Rubies

The Poetry Posse 2015
Jamie Bond * Gail Weston Shazor * Albert 'Infinite' Carrasco
Siddartha Beth Pierce * Janet P. Caldwell * Tony Henninger
Joe DaVerbal Minddancer * Neetu Wali * Shareef Abdur – Rasheed
Kimberly Burnham * Ann White * Keith Alan Hamilton
Katherine Wyatt * Fahredin Shehu * Hülya N. Yılmaz
Teresa E. Gallion * Jackie Allen * William S. Peters, Sr.

The Year of the Poet II
August 2015

Peridot

Featured Poets
Gayle Howell
Ann Chalasz
Christopher Schultz

The Poetry Posse 2015
Jamie Bond * Gail Weston Shazor * Albert 'Infinite' Carrasco
Siddartha Beth Pierce * Janet P. Caldwell * Tony Henninger
Joe DaVerbal Minddancer * Neetu Wali * Shareef Abdur – Rasheed
Kimberly Burnham * Ann White * Keith Alan Hamilton
Katherine Wyatt * Fahredin Shehu * Hülya N. Yılmaz
Teresa E. Gallion * Jackie Allen * William S. Peters, Sr.

Now Available

www.innerchildpress.com/the-year-of-the-poet

The Year of the Poet II
September 2015

Featured Poets
Alfreda Ghee * Lonneice Weeks Badley * Demetrios Trifiatis

Sapphires

The Poetry Posse 2015
Jamie Bond * Gail Weston Shazor * Albert 'Infinite' Carrasco
Siddartha Beth Pierce * Janet P. Caldwell * Tony Henninger
Joe DaVerbal Minddancer * Neetu Wali * Shareef Abdur – Rasheed
Kimberly Burnham * Ann White * Keith Alan Hamilton
Katherine Wyatt * Fahredin Shehu * Hülya N. Yılmaz
Teresa E. Gallion * Jackie Allen * William S. Peters, Sr.

The Year of the Poet II
October 2015

Featured Poets
Monte Smith * Laura J. Wolfe * William Washington

Opal

The Poetry Posse 2015
Jamie Bond * Gail Weston Shazor * Albert 'Infinite' Carrasco
Siddartha Beth Pierce * Janet P. Caldwell * Tony Henninger
Joe DaVerbal Minddancer * Neetu Wali * Shareef Abdur – Rasheed
Kimberly Burnham * Ann White * Keith Alan Hamilton
Katherine Wyatt * Fahredin Shehu * Hülya N. Yılmaz
Teresa E. Gallion * Jackie Allen * William S. Peters, Sr.

The Year of the Poet II
November 2015

Featured Poets
Alan W. Jankowski
Bismay Mohanty
James Moore

Topaz

The Poetry Posse 2015
Jamie Bond * Gail Weston Shazor * Albert 'Infinite' Carrasco
Siddartha Beth Pierce * Janet P. Caldwell * Tony Henninger
Joe DaVerbal Minddancer * Neetu Wali * Shareef Abdur – Rasheed
Kimberly Burnham * Ann White * Keith Alan Hamilton
Katherine Wyatt * Fahredin Shehu * Hülya N. Yılmaz
Teresa E. Gallion * Jackie Allen * William S. Peters, Sr.

The Year of the Poet II
December 2015

Featured Poets
Kerione Bryan * Michelle Joan Barulich * Neville Hiatt

Turquoise

The Poetry Posse 2015
Jamie Bond * Gail Weston Shazor * Albert 'Infinite' Carrasco
Siddartha Beth Pierce * Janet P. Caldwell * Tony Henninger
Joe DaVerbal Minddancer * Neetu Wali * Shareef Abdur – Rasheed
Kimberly Burnham * Ann White * Keith Alan Hamilton
Katherine Wyatt * Fahredin Shehu * Hülya N. Yılmaz
Teresa E. Gallion * Jackie Allen * William S. Peters, Sr.

Now Available

www.innerchildpress.com/the-year-of-the-poet

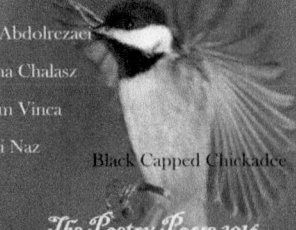

The Year of the Poet
May 2016

Bob Strum
Barbara Allan
D.L. Davis

Oriole

The Poetry Posse 2016

The Year of the Poet III
June 2016

Featured Poets

Qibrije Demiri- Frangu
Naime Beqiraj
Faleeha Hassan
Bedri Zyberaj

Black Necked Stilt

The Poetry Posse 2016

The Year of the Poet III
July 2016

Featured Poets

Tram Fatima 'Ashi
Langley Shazor
Jody Doty
Emilia T. Davis

Indigo Bunting

The Poetry Posse 2016

The Year of the Poet III
August 2016

Featured Poets

Anita Dash
Irena Jovanovic
Malgorzata Gouluda

Painted Bunting

The Poetry Posse 2016

Now Available
www.innerchildpress.com/the-year-of-the-poet

223

The Year of the Poet III
September 2016

Featured Poets
Simone Weber
Abhijit Sen
Eunice Barbara C. Novio

Long Billed Curle

The Poetry Posse 2016

The Year of the Poet III
October 2016

Featured Poets
Lana Joseph
Indra Krishnamurthy R
James Moore

Barn Owl

The Poetry Posse 2016

The Year of the Poet III
November 2016

Featured Poets
Rosemary Burns
Robin Ouzman Hislop
Lonneice Weeks-Badler

Northern Cardinal

The Poetry Posse 2016

Gail Weston Shazor * Caroline Nazareno * Jen Walls
Nizar Sartawi * Janet P. Caldwell * Alfredo Ghee
Joe DeVerbel Minddancer * Shareef Abdur – Rasheed
Albert Carrasco * Kimberly Burnham * Elizabeth Castillo
Hülya N. Yılmaz * Demetrios Trifiatis * Alan W. Jankowski
Teresa E. Gallion * Jackie Davis Allen * William S. Peters, Sr

The Year of the Poet III
December 2016

Featured Poets
Samih Masoud
Mountassir Aziz Bien
Abdulkadir Musa

Rough Legged Hawk

The Poetry Posse 2016

Now Available

www.innerchildpress.com/the-year-of-the-poet

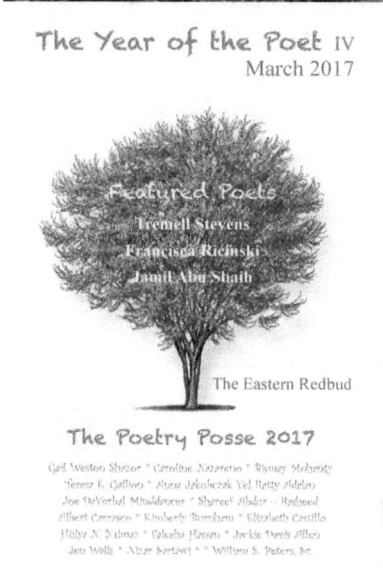

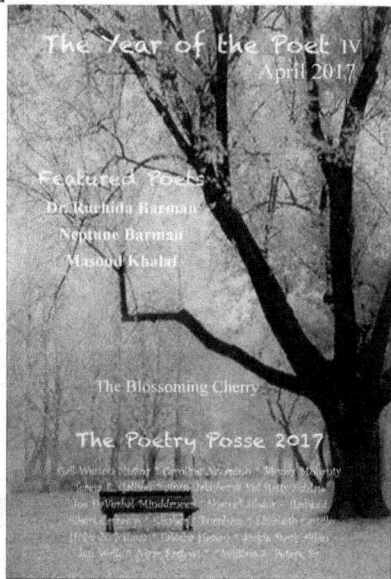

The Year of the Poet IV — January 2017
Featured Poets: Jon Winell, Natalie Shields, Irani Fatima Ashi
Quaking Aspen
The Poetry Posse 2017

The Year of the Poet IV — February 2017
Featured Poets: Lin Ross, Souhaina Fathi, Anwer Ghani
Witch Hazel
The Poetry Posse 2017

The Year of the Poet IV — March 2017
Featured Poets: Tremell Stevens, Francisca Ricinski, Jamil Abu Shaib
The Eastern Redbud
The Poetry Posse 2017

The Year of the Poet IV — April 2017
Featured Poets: Dr. Ruchida Barman, Neptune Barman, Masood Khalaf
The Blossoming Cherry
The Poetry Posse 2017

Now Available

www.innerchildpress.com/the-year-of-the-poet

The Year of the Poet IV
May 2017

The Flowering Dogwood Tree

Featured Poets
Kallisa Powell
Alieja Maria Kuberska
Fethi Sassi

The Poetry Posse 2017

Gail Weston Shazor * Caroline Nazareno * Bismay Mohanty
Teresa E. Gallion * Anne Jakubczak Vel Ratty Adalan
Joe DaVerbal Minddancer * Shareef Abdur – Rasheed
Albert Carrasco * Kimberly Burnham * Elizabeth Castillo
Hülya N. Yılmaz * Telosha Henson * Jackie Davis Allen
Jen Walls * Nizar Sartawi * * William S. Peters, Sr.

The Year of the Poet IV
June 2017

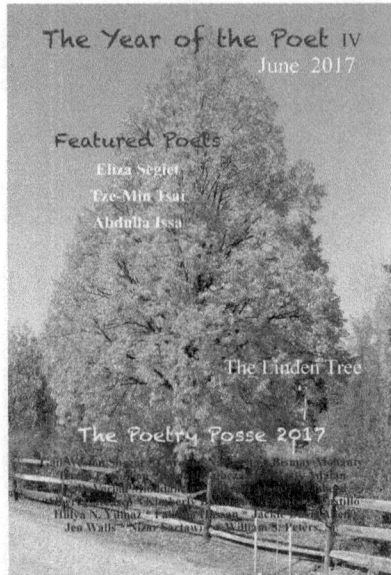

Featured Poets
Eliza Segiet
Tze-Min Tsai
Abdulla Issa

The Linden Tree

The Poetry Posse 2017

Jen Walls * Nizar Sartawi * * William S. Peters, Sr.

The Year of the Poet IV
July 2017

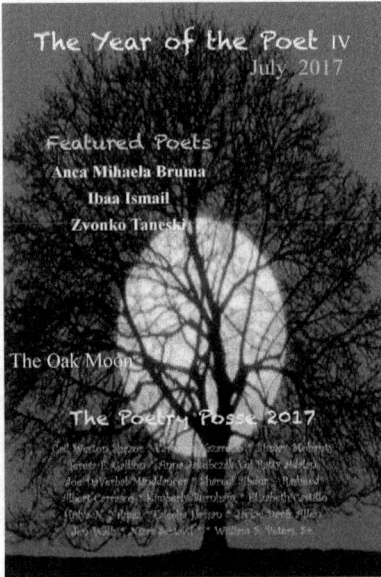

Featured Poets
Anca Mihaela Bruma
Ibaa Ismail
Zvonko Taneski

The Oak Moon

The Poetry Posse 2017

The Year of the Poet IV
August 2017

Featured Poets
Jonathan Aquino
Kitty Hsu
Langley Shazor

The Hazelnut Tree

The Poetry Posse 2017

Gail Weston Shazor * Caroline Nazareno *
Teresa E. Gallion * Anne Jakubczak Vel Ratty Adalan
Joe DaVerbal Minddancer * Shareef Abdur – Rasheed
Albert Carrasco * Kimberly Burnham * Elizabeth Castillo
Hülya N. Yılmaz * Telosha Henson * Jackie Davis Allen
Jen Walls * Nizar Sartawi * * William S. Peters, Sr.

Now Available

www.innerchildpress.com/the-year-of-the-poet

The Year of the Poet IV
September 2017

Featured Poets

Martina Reisz Newberry
Ameer Nassir
Christine Fulco Neal
Robert Neal

The Elm Tree

The Poetry Posse 2017

Gail Weston Shazor * Caroline Nazareno * Bismay Mohanty
Teresa E. Gallion * Anna Jakubczak Vel Ratty Adalan
Joe DaVerbal Minddancer * Shareef Abdur – Rasheed
Albert Carrasco * Kimberly Burnham * Elizabeth Castillo
Hülya N. Yılmaz * Faleeha Hassan * Jackie Davis Allen
Jen Walls * Nizar Sartawi * * William S. Peters, Sr.

The Year of the Poet IV
October 2017

Featured Poets

Ahmed Abu Saleem
Nedal Al-Qaeim
Sadeddin Shahin

The Black Walnut Tree

The Poetry Posse 2017

Gail Weston Shazor * Caroline Nazareno * Bismay Mohanty
Teresa E. Gallion * Anna Jakubczak Vel Ratty Adalan
Joe DaVerbal Minddancer * Shareef Abdur – Rasheed
Albert Carrasco * Kimberly Burnham * Elizabeth Castillo
Hülya N. Yılmaz * Faleeha Hassan * Jackie Davis Allen
Jen Walls * Nizar Sartawi * * William S. Peters, Sr.

The Year of the Poet IV
November 2017

Featured Poets

Kay Peters
Alfreda D. Ghee
Gabriella Garofalo
Rosemary Cappello

The Tree of Life

The Poetry Posse 2017

Gail Weston Shazor * Caroline Nazareno * Bismay Mohanty
Teresa E. Gallion * Anna Jakubczak Vel Ratty Adalan
Joe DaVerbal Minddancer * Shareef Abdur – Rasheed
Albert Carrasco * Kimberly Burnham * Elizabeth Castillo
Hülya N. Yılmaz * Faleeha Hassan * Jackie Davis Allen
Jen Walls * Nizar Sartawi * William S. Peters, Sr.

The Year of the Poet IV
December 2017

Featured Poets

Justice Clarke
Mariel M. Pabroa
Kiley Brown

The Fig Tree

The Poetry Posse 2017

Gail Weston Shazor * Caroline Nazareno * Bismay Mohanty
Teresa E. Gallion * Anna Jakubczak Vel Ratty Adalan
Joe DaVerbal Minddancer * Shareef Abdur – Rasheed
Albert Carrasco * Kimberly Burnham * Elizabeth Castillo
Hülya N. Yılmaz * Faleeha Hassan * Jackie Davis Allen
Jen Walls * Nizar Sartawi * William S. Peters, Sr.

Now Available

www.innerchildpress.com/the-year-of-the-poet

The Year of the Poet V
January 2018

Featured Poets

Iyad Shamasnah

Yasmeen Hamzeh

Ali Abdolrezaei

Aksum

The Poetry Posse 2018

Gail Weston Shazor * Caroline Nazareno * Tezmin Ition Tsai
Hülya N. Yılmaz * Faleeha Hassan * Jackie Davis Allen
Teresa E. Gallion * Anna Jakubczak Vel Ratty Adalan
Alicja Maria Kuberska * Shareef Abdur – Rasheed
Kimberly Burnham * Elizabeth Castillo
Nizar Sartawi * William S. Peters, Sr.

The Year of the Poet V
February 2018

Sabean

Featured Poets

Muhammad Azram

Anna Szawracka

Abhilipsa Kuanar

Aanika Aery

The Poetry Posse 2018

Gail Weston Shazor * Caroline Nazareno * Tezmin Ition Tsai
Hülya N. Yılmaz * Faleeha Hassan * Jackie Davis Allen
Teresa E. Gallion * Anna Jakubczak Vel Ratty Adalan
Alicja Maria Kuberska * Shareef Abdur – Rasheed
Kimberly Burnham * Elizabeth Castillo
Nizar Sartawi * William S. Peters, Sr.

The Year of the Poet V
March 2018

Featured Poets

Iram Fatima 'Ashi'
Cassandra Swan
Jaleel Khazaal
Sharia Zaman

Mexico
Cuba
Dominican Republic
Belize
Jamaica
Haiti
Puerto Rico
Guatemala
Honduras
El Salvador
Nicaragua
Costa Rica
Panama
Colombia

Caribbean
&
Middle America

The Poetry Posse 2018

Gail Weston Shazor * Nizar Sartawi * Hülya N. Yılmaz
Jackie Davis Allen * Caroline 'Ceri' Nazareno
Alicja Maria Kuberska * Teresa E. Gallion
Faleeha Hassan * Shareef Abdur – Rasheed
Kimberly Burnham * Elizabeth Castillo
Tezmin Ition Tsai * William S. Peters, Sr.

The Year of the Poet V
April 2018

Featured Poets

The Nez Perce

The Poetry Posse 2018

Now Available

www.innerchildpress.com/the-year-of-the-poet

The Year of the Poet V
May 2018

Featured Poets

Zsldy Carrion de Leon Jr.
Sylwia K. Malinowska
Lsadita Altrineti
Ofelia Prodan

The Sumerians

The Poetry Posse 2018

Gail Weston Shazor * Nizar Sartawi * Hülya N. Yılmaz
Jackie Davis Allen * Caroline 'Ceri' Nazareno
Alicja Maria Kuberska * Teresa E. Gallion
Kimberly Burnham * Shareef Abdur – Rasheed
Faleeha Hassan * Elizabeth Castillo * Swapna Behera
Tezmin Ition Tsai * William S. Peters, Sr.

The Year of the Poet V
June 2018

Featured Poets

Bilall Maliqi * Daim Miftari * Gojko Božović * Sofija Živković

The Paleo Indians

The Poetry Posse 2018

Gail Weston Shazor * Nizar Sartawi * Hülya N. Yılmaz
Jackie Davis Allen * Caroline 'Ceri' Nazareno
Alicja Maria Kuberska * Teresa E. Gallion
Kimberly Burnham * Shareef Abdur – Rasheed
Faleeha Hassan * Elizabeth Castillo * Swapna Behera
Tezmin Ition Tsai * William S. Peters, Sr.

The Year of the Poet V
July 2018

Featured Poets

Padmaja Iyengar-Paddy
Mohammad Ikbal Hazit
Eliza Segiet
Tom Higgins

Oceania

The Poetry Posse 2018

Gail Weston Shazor * Nizar Sartawi * Hülya N. Yılmaz
Jackie Davis Allen * Caroline 'Ceri' Nazareno
Alicja Maria Kuberska * Teresa E. Gallion
Kimberly Burnham * Shareef Abdur – Rasheed
Faleeha Hassan * Elizabeth Castillo * Swapna Behera
Tezmin Ition Tsai * William S. Peters, Sr.

The Year of the Poet V
August 2018

Featured Poets
Hussein Habasch * Mircea Dan Duta * Naida Mujkić * Swagat Das

The Lapita

The Poetry Posse 2018

Gail Weston Shazor * Nizar Sartawi * Hülya N. Yılmaz
Jackie Davis Allen * Caroline 'Ceri' Nazareno
Alicja Maria Kuberska * Teresa E. Gallion
Kimberly Burnham * Shareef Abdur – Rasheed
Ashok K. Bhargava* Elizabeth Castillo * Swapna Behaera
Tezmin Ition Tsai * William S. Peters, Sr.

Now Available
www.innerchildpress.com/the-year-of-the-poet

The Year of the Poet V
September 2018

The Aztecs & Incas

Featured Poets
Kolade Olanrewaju Freedom
Eliza Segiet
Mesker Hassen Abdul Ghani
Lily Swarn

The Poetry Posse 2018

Gail Weston Shazor * Nizar Sartawi * Hülya N. Yılmaz
Jackie Davis Allen * Caroline 'Ceri' Nazareno
Alicja Maria Kuberska * Teresa E. Gallion
Kimberly Burnham * Shareef Abdur – Rasheed
Ashok K. Bhargava * Elizabeth Castillo * Swapna Behera
Tezmin Ition Tsai * William S. Peters, Sr.

The Year of the Poet V
October 2018

Featured Poets
Alicia Minjarez * Lonneice Weeks-Badley
Lopamudra Mishra * Abdelwahed Souayah

Bengali

The Poetry Posse 2018

Gail Weston Shazor * Nizar Sartawi * Hülya N. Yılmaz
Jackie Davis Allen * Caroline 'Ceri' Nazareno
Alicja Maria Kuberska * Teresa E. Gallion
Kimberly Burnham * Shareef Abdur – Rasheed
Ashok K. Bhargava * Elizabeth Castillo * Swapna Behera
Tezmin Ition Tsai * William S. Peters, Sr.

The Year of the Poet V
November 2018

Featured Poets
Michelle Joan Barulich * Monsif Beroual
Krystyna Konecka * Nassira Nezzar

The Poetry Posse 2018

Gail Weston Shazor * Nizar Sartawi * Hülya N. Yılmaz
Jackie Davis Allen * Caroline 'Ceri' Nazareno
Alicja Maria Kuberska * Teresa E. Gallion
Kimberly Burnham * Shareef Abdur – Rasheed
Ashok K. Bhargava * Elizabeth Castillo * Swapna Behera
Tezmin Ition Tsai * William S. Peters, Sr.

The Year of the Poet V
December 2018

Featured Poets
Rose Terranova Cirigliano
Joanna Kalinowska
Sokolović Emin
Dr. T. Ashok Chakravarthy

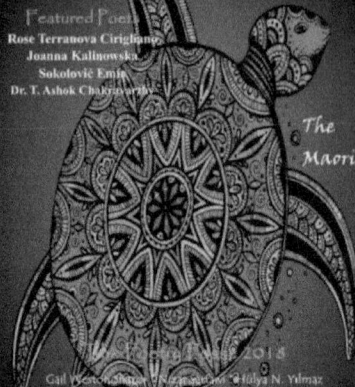

The Maori

The Poetry Posse 2018

Gail Weston Shazor * Nizar Sartawi * Hülya N. Yılmaz
Jackie Davis Allen * Caroline 'Ceri' Nazareno
Alicja Maria Kuberska * Teresa E. Gallion
Kimberly Burnham * Shareef Abdur – Rasheed
Ashok K. Bhargava * Elizabeth Castillo * Swapna Behera
Tezmin Ition Tsai * William S. Peters, Sr.

Now Available

www.innerchildpress.com/the-year-of-the-poet

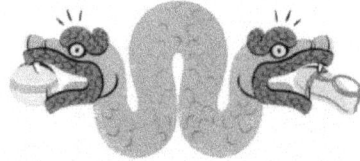

The Year of the Poet VI
May 2019

Featured Poets

Emad Al-Haydary * Hussein Nasser Jabr
Wahab Sheriff * Abdul Razzaq Al Ameeri

Asia Southeast Asia and Maritime Asia

The Poetry Posse 2019

Gail Weston Shazor * Albert Carrasco * Hülya N. Yılmaz
Jackie Davis Allen * Caroline Nazareno * Eliza Segiet
Alicja Maria Kuberska * Teresa E. Gallion * Joe Paire
Kimberly Burnham * Shareef Abdur – Rasheed
Ashok K. Bhargava * Elizabeth Castillo * Swapna Behera
Tezmin Ition Tsai * William S. Peters, Sr.

The Year of the Poet VI
June 2019

Featured Poets

Kate Gaudi Powiekszone * Sahaj Sabharwal
Iwu Jeff * Mohamed Abdel Aziz Shmeis

Arctic
Circumpolar

The Poetry Posse 2019

Gail Weston Shazor * Albert Carrasco * Hülya N. Yılmaz
Jackie Davis Allen * Caroline Nazareno * Eliza Segiet
Alicja Maria Kuberska * Teresa E. Gallion * Joe Paire
Kimberly Burnham * Shareef Abdur – Rasheed
Ashok K. Bhargava * Elizabeth Castillo * Swapna Behera
Tezmin Ition Tsai * William S. Peters, Sr.

The Year of the Poet VI
July 2019

Featured Poets

Saadeddin Shabio   Andy Scott
Fahredin Shehu   Alok Kumar Ray

The Horn of Africa

Ethiopia   Djibouti

Somalia   Eritrea

The Poetry Posse 2019

Gail Weston Shazor * Albert Carrasco * Hülya N. Yılmaz
Jackie Davis Allen * Caroline Nazareno * Eliza Segiet
Alicja Maria Kuberska * Teresa E. Gallion * Joe Paire
Kimberly Burnham * Shareef Abdur – Rasheed
Ashok K. Bhargava * Elizabeth Castillo * Swapna Behera
Tezmin Ition Tsai * William S. Peters, Sr.

The Year of the Poet VI
August 2019

Featured Poets

Shola Balogun * Bharati Nayak
Monalisa Dash Dwibedy * Mbizo Chirasha

Coexist

Southwest Asia

The Poetry Posse 2019

Gail Weston Shazor * Albert Carrasco * Hülya N. Yılmaz
Jackie Davis Allen * Caroline Nazareno * Eliza Segiet
Alicja Maria Kuberska * Teresa E. Gallion * Joe Paire
Kimberly Burnham * Shareef Abdur – Rasheed
Ashok K. Bhargava * Elizabeth Castillo * Swapna Behera
Tezmin Ition Tsai * William S. Peters, Sr.

Now Available

www.innerchildpress.com/the-year-of-the-poet

The Year of the Poet VI
September 2019
Featured Poets
Elena Liliana Popescu * Gobinda Biswas
Irma Fatima 'Ashi' * Joseph S. Spence, Sr

The Caucasus
The Poetry Posse 2019
Gail Weston Shazor * Albert Carasco * Hülya N. Yilmaz
Jackie Davis Allen * Caroline Nazareno * Eliza Segiet
Alicja Maria Kuberska * Teresa E. Gallion * Joe Paire
Kimberly Burnham * Shareef Abdur – Rasheed
Ashok K. Bhargava * Elizabeth Castillo * Swapna Behera
Tezmin Ition Tsai * William S. Peters, Sr

The Year of the Poet VI
October 2019
Featured Poets
Ngozi Olivia Osuoha * Denisa Kondić
Pankhuri Sinha * Christena AV Williams

The Nile Valley
The Poetry Posse 2019
Gail Weston Shazor * Albert Carasco * Hülya N. Yilmaz
Jackie Davis Allen * Caroline Nazareno * Eliza Segiet
Alicja Maria Kuberska * Teresa E. Gallion * Joe Paire
Kimberly Burnham * Shareef Abdur – Rasheed
Ashok K. Bhargava * Elizabeth Castillo * Swapna Behera
Tezmin Ition Tsai * William S. Peters, Sr

The Year of the Poet VI
November 2019
Featured Poets
Rozalia Aleksandrova * Orbindu Ganga
Smruti Ranjan Mohanty * Sofia Skleida

Northern Asia
The Poetry Posse 2019
Gail Weston Shazor * Albert Carasco * Hülya N. Yilmaz
Jackie Davis Allen * Caroline Nazareno * Eliza Segiet
Aicja Maria Kuberska * Teresa E. Gallion * Joe Paire
Kimberly Burnham * Shareef Abdur – Rasheed
Ashok K. Bhargava * Elizabeth Castillo * Swapna Behera
Tezmin Ition Tsai * William S. Peters, Sr

The Year of the Poet VI
December 2019
Featured Poets
Bishop Karlos (Karimou) * Sujata Paul
Bharati Nayak * Kaparidei Olivieta

Oceania
The Poetry Posse 2019
Gail Weston Shazor * Albert Carasco * Hülya N. Yilmaz
Jackie Davis Allen * Caroline Nazareno * Eliza Segiet
Aicja Maria Kuberska * Teresa E. Gallion * Joe Paire
Kimberly Burnham * Shareef Abdur – Rasheed
Ashok K. Bhargava * Elizabeth Castillo * Swapna Behera
Tezmin Ition Tsai * William S. Peters, Sr

Now Available
www.innerchildpress.com/the-year-of-the-poet

The Year of the Poet VII
January 2020

Featured Poets
B S Tyagi * Ashok Chakravarthy Tholana
Andy Scott * Anwer Ghani

1901 Jean Henry Dunant and Frédéric Passy

The Year of Peace
Celebrating past Nobel Peace Prize Recipients

The Poetry Posse 2020
Gail Weston Shazor * Albert Carasco * Hülya N. Yilmaz
Jackie Davis Allen * Caroline Nazareno * Eliza Segiet
Alicja Maria Kuberska * Teresa E. Gallion * Joe Paire
Kimberly Burnham * Shareef Abdur – Rasheed
Ashok K. Bhargava * Elizabeth Castillo * Swapna Behera
Tezmin Ition Tsai * William S. Peters, Sr.

The Year of the Poet VII
February 2020

Featured Poets
Jennifer Ades * Martina Reisz Newberry
Ibrahim Honjo * Claudia Piccinno

Henri La Fontaine ~ 1913

The Year of Peace
Celebrating past Nobel Peace Prize Recipients

The Poetry Posse 2020
Gail Weston Shazor * Albert Carasco * Hülya N. Yilmaz
Jackie Davis Allen * Caroline Nazareno * Eliza Segiet
Alicja Maria Kuberska * Teresa E. Gallion * Joe Paire
Kimberly Burnham * Shareef Abdur – Rasheed
Ashok K. Bhargava * Elizabeth Castillo * Swapna Behera
Tezmin Ition Tsai * William S. Peters, Sr.

The Year of the Poet VII
March 2020

Featured Poets
Azuz Mountassir * Krishna Paraisa
Hannie Rouweler * Rozalia Aleksandrova

Aristide Briand ~ 1926 ~ Gustav Stresemann

The Year of Peace
Celebrating past Nobel Peace Prize Recipients

The Poetry Posse 2020
Gail Weston Shazor * Albert Carasco * Hülya N. Yilmaz
Jackie Davis Allen * Caroline Nazareno * Eliza Segiet
Alicja Maria Kuberska * Teresa E. Gallion * Joe Paire
Kimberly Burnham * Shareef Abdur – Rasheed
Ashok K. Bhargava * Elizabeth Castillo * Swapna Behera
Tezmin Ition Tsai * William S. Peters, Sr.

The Year of the Poet VII
April 2020

Featured Poets
Rohini Behera * Mircea Dan Duta
Monalisa Dash Dwibedy * NilavroNill Shoovro

Carlos Saavedra Lamas ~ 1936

The Year of Peace
Celebrating past Nobel Peace Prize Recipients

The Poetry Posse 2020
Gail Weston Shazor * Albert Carasco * Hülya N. Yilmaz
Jackie Davis Allen * Caroline Nazareno * Eliza Segiet
Alicja Maria Kuberska * Teresa E. Gallion * Joe Paire
Kimberly Burnham * Shareef Abdur – Rasheed
Ashok K. Bhargava * Elizabeth Castillo * Swapna Behera
Tezmin Ition Tsai * William S. Peters, Sr.

Now Available

www.innerchildpress.com/the-year-of-the-poet

The Year of the Poet VII

May 2020

Featured Poets
Alok Kumar Ray * Eden S. Trinidad
Franco Barbato * Izabela Zubko

Ralph Bunche ~ 1950

The Year of Peace
Celebrating past Nobel Peace Prize Recipients

The Poetry Posse 2020

Gail Weston Shazor * Albert Carrasco * Hülya N. Yılmaz
Jackie Davis Allen * Caroline Nazareno * Eliza Segiet
Alicja Maria Kubeńska * Teresa E. Gallion * Joe Paire
Kimberly Burnham * Shareef Abdur – Rasheed
Ashok K. Bhargava * Elizabeth Castillo * Swapna Behera
Tezmin Ition Tsai * William S. Peters, Sr.

The Year of the Poet VII

June 2020

Featured Poets
Eftichia Kapardeli * Metin Cengiz
Hussein Habasch * Kosh K Mathew

Albert John Lutuli ~ 1960

The Year of Peace
Celebrating past Nobel Peace Prize Recipients

The Poetry Posse 2020

Gail Weston Shazor * Albert Carrasco * Hülya N. Yılmaz
Jackie Davis Allen * Caroline Nazareno * Eliza Segiet
Alicja Maria Kubeńska * Teresa E. Gallion * Joe Paire
Kimberly Burnham * Shareef Abdur – Rasheed
Ashok K. Bhargava * Elizabeth Castillo * Swapna Behera
Tezmin Ition Tsai * William S. Peters, Sr.

The Year of the Poet VII

July 2020

Featured Poets
Mykola Martyniuk * Orbindu Ganga
Roula Pollard * Karn Praktisha

Norman Ernest Borlaug ~ 1970

The Year of Peace
Celebrating past Nobel Peace Prize Recipients

The Poetry Posse 2020

Gail Weston Shazor * Albert Carrasco * Hülya N. Yılmaz
Jackie Davis Allen * Caroline Nazareno * Eliza Segiet
Alicja Maria Kubeńska * Teresa E. Gallion * Joe Paire
Kimberly Burnham * Shareef Abdur – Rasheed
Ashok K. Bhargava * Elizabeth Castillo * Swapna Behera
Tezmin Ition Tsai * William S. Peters, Sr.

The Year of the Poet VII

August 2020

Featured Poets
Dr Pragya Suman * Chinh Nguyen
Srinivas Vasudev * Ugwu Leonard Ifeanyi, Jr.

Adolfo Pérez Esquivel ~ 1980

The Year of Peace
Celebrating past Nobel Peace Prize Recipients

The Poetry Posse 2020

Gail Weston Shazor * Albert Carrasco * Hülya N. Yılmaz
Jackie Davis Allen * Caroline Nazareno * Eliza Segiet
Alicja Maria Kubeńska * Teresa E. Gallion * Joe Paire
Kimberly Burnham * Shareef Abdur – Rasheed
Ashok K. Bhargava * Elizabeth Castillo * Swapna Behera
Tezmin Ition Tsai * William S. Peters, Sr.

Now Available

www.innerchildpress.com/the-year-of-the-poet

The Year of the Poet VII
September 2020

Featured Poets
Raod Anis Al-Jishi • Sotkonovic Snezana
Dr. Brajesh Kumar Gupta • Umid Najari

Mikhail Sergeyevich Gorbachev ~ 1990

The Year of Peace
Celebrating past Nobel Peace Prize Recipients

The Poetry Posse 2020
Gail Weston Shazor • Albert Carasco • Hülya N. Yılmaz
Jackie Davis Allen • Caroline Nazareno • Eliza Segiet
Alicja Maria Kuberska • Teresa E. Gallion • Joe Paire
Kimberly Burnham • Shareef Abdur – Rasheed
Ashok K. Bhargava • Elizabeth Castillo • Swapna Behera
Tezmin Ition Tsai • William S. Peters, Sr.

The Year of the Poet VII
October 2020

Featured Poets
Mutawaf A. Shaheed • Galina Italyanskaya
Nadeem Fraz • Avril Tanya Meallem

Kim Dae-jung ~ 2000

The Year of Peace
Celebrating past Nobel Peace Prize Recipients

The Poetry Posse 2020
Gail Weston Shazor • Albert Carasco • Hülya N. Yılmaz
Jackie Davis Allen • Caroline Nazareno • Eliza Segiet
Alicja Maria Kuberska • Teresa E. Gallion • Joe Paire
Kimberly Burnham • Shareef Abdur – Rasheed
Ashok K. Bhargava • Elizabeth Castillo • Swapna Behera
Tezmin Ition Tsai • William S. Peters, Sr.

The Year of the Poet VII
November 2020

Featured Poets
Elisa Mason • Sue Lindenberg McClelland
Hatif Janabi • Ivan Gaćina

Liu Xiaobo ~ 2010

The Year of Peace
Celebrating past Nobel Peace Prize Recipients

The Poetry Posse 2020
Gail Weston Shazor • Albert Carasco • Hülya N. Yılmaz
Jackie Davis Allen • Caroline Nazareno • Eliza Segiet
Alicja Maria Kuberska • Teresa E. Gallion • Joe Paire
Kimberly Burnham • Shareef Abdur – Rasheed
Ashok K. Bhargava • Elizabeth Castillo • Swapna Behera
Tezmin Ition Tsai • William S. Peters, Sr.

The Year of the Poet VII
December 2020

Featured Poets
Ratan Ghosh • Ibtisam Ibrahim Al-Asady
Brindha Vinodh • Selma Kopic

Abiy Ahmed Ali ~ 2019

The Year of Peace
Celebrating past Nobel Peace Prize Recipients

The Poetry Posse 2020
Gail Weston Shazor • Albert Carasco • Hülya N. Yılmaz
Jackie Davis Allen • Caroline Nazareno • Eliza Segiet
Alicja Maria Kuberska • Teresa E. Gallion • Joe Paire
Kimberly Burnham • Shareef Abdur – Rasheed
Ashok K. Bhargava • Elizabeth Castillo • Swapna Behera
Tezmin Ition Tsai • William S. Peters, Sr.

Now Available

www.innerchildpress.com/the-year-of-the-poet

The Year of the Poet VIII

January 2021

Featured Global Poets
Andrew Scott * Debaprasanna Biswas
Shakil Kalam * Changming Yuan

Banksy's The Girl with the Pierced Eardrum

Poetry ... Ekphrasticly Speaking
The Poetry Posse 2020
Gail Weston Shazor * Albert Carasco * Hülya N. Yilmaz
Jackie Davis Allen * Caroline Nazareno * Eliza Segiet
Alicja Maria Kuberska * Teresa E. Gallion * Joe Paire
Kimberly Burnham * Shareef Abdur – Rasheed
Ashok K. Bhargava * Elizabeth Castillo * Swapna Behera
Tezmin Ition Tsai * William S. Peters, Sr.

The Year of the Poet VIII

February 2021

Featured Global Poets
T. Ramesh Babu * Ruchida Barman
Neptune Barman * Faleeha Hassan

Emory Douglas : 1968 Olympics mural

Poetry ... Ekphrasticly Speaking
The Poetry Posse 2021
Gail Weston Shazor * Albert Carasco * Hülya N. Yilmaz
Jackie Davis Allen * Caroline Nazareno * Eliza Segiet
Alicja Maria Kuberska * Teresa E. Gallion * Joe Paire
Kimberly Burnham * Shareef Abdur – Rasheed
Ashok K. Bhargava * Elizabeth Castillo * Swapna Behera
Tezmin Ition Tsai * William S. Peters, Sr.

The Year of the Poet VIII

March 2021

Featured Global Poets
Claudia Piccinno * Mohammed Jabr
Luzviminda Rivera *Nigar Arif

Tatyana Fazlalizadeh

Poetry ... Ekphrasticly Speaking
The Poetry Posse 2021
Gail Weston Shazor * Albert Carasco * Hülya N. Yilmaz
Jackie Davis Allen * Caroline Nazareno * Eliza Segiet
Alicja Maria Kuberska * Teresa E. Gallion * Joe Paire
Kimberly Burnham * Shareef Abdur – Rasheed
Ashok K. Bhargava * Elizabeth Castillo * Swapna Behera
Tezmin Ition Tsai * William S. Peters, Sr.

The Year of the Poet VIII

April 2021

Featured Global Poets
Katarzyna Brus- Sawczuk * Anwesha Paul
Rozalia Aleksandrova * Shahid Abbas

Pablo O'Higgins

Poetry ... Ekphrasticly Speaking
The Poetry Posse 2021
Gail Weston Shazor * Albert Carasco * Hülya N. Yilmaz
Jackie Davis Allen * Caroline Nazareno * Eliza Segiet
Alicja Maria Kuberska * Teresa E. Gallion * Joe Paire
Kimberly Burnham * Shareef Abdur – Rasheed
Ashok K. Bhargava * Elizabeth Castillo * Swapna Behera
Tezmin Ition Tsai * William S. Peters, Sr.

Now Available

www.innerchildpress.com/the-year-of-the-poet

The Year of the Poet VIII
May 2021

Featured Global Poets
Paramita Mukherjee Mullick * Rose Zerguine
Jaydeep Sarangi * Bismay Mohanty

Diego Rivera

Poetry ... Ekphrasticly Speaking

The Poetry Posse 2021
Gail Weston Shazor * Albert Carasco * Hülya N. Yılmaz
Jackie Davis Allen * Caroline Nazareno * Eliza Segiet
Alicja Maria Kuberska * Teresa E. Gallion * Joe Paire
Kimberly Burnham * Shareef Abdur – Rasheed
Ashok K. Bhargava * Elizabeth Castillo * Swapna Behera
Tezmin Ition Tsai * William S. Peters, Sr.

The Year of the Poet VIII
June 2021

Featured Global Poets
Alonzo "zO" Gross * Lali Tsipi Michaeli
Tareq al Karmy * Tirthendu Ganguly

Rayen Kang

Poetry ... Ekphrasticly Speaking

The Poetry Posse 2021
Gail Weston Shazor * Albert Carasco * Hülya N. Yılmaz
Jackie Davis Allen * Caroline Nazareno * Eliza Segiet
Alicja Maria Kuberska * Teresa E. Gallion * Joe Paire
Kimberly Burnham * Shareef Abdur – Rasheed
Ashok K. Bhargava * Elizabeth Castillo * Swapna Behera
Tezmin Ition Tsai * William S. Peters, Sr.

The Year of the Poet VIII
July 2021

Featured Global Poets
Iram Jaan * Vesna Mundishevska-Veljanovska
Ngozi Olivia Osuoha * Lan Qyqalla

Goncalao Mabunda

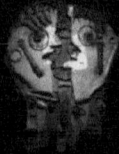

Poetry ... Ekphrasticly Speaking

The Poetry Posse 2021
Gail Weston Shazor * Albert Carasco * Hülya N. Yılmaz
Jackie Davis Allen * Caroline Nazareno * Eliza Segiet
Alicja Maria Kuberska * Teresa E. Gallion * Joe Paire
Kimberly Burnham * Shareef Abdur – Rasheed
Ashok K. Bhargava * Elizabeth Castillo * Swapna Behera
Tezmin Ition Tsai * William S. Peters, Sr.

The Year of the Poet VIII
August 2021

Featured Global Poets
Caroline Laurent Turunc * Kamal Dhungana
Pankhuri Sinha * Paramita Mukherjee Mullick

Mundara Koorang

Poetry ... Ekphrasticly Speaking

The Poetry Posse 2021
Gail Weston Shazor * Albert Carasco * Hülya N. Yılmaz
Jackie Davis Allen * Caroline Nazareno * Eliza Segiet
Alicja Maria Kuberska * Teresa E. Gallion * Joe Paire
Kimberly Burnham * Shareef Abdur – Rasheed
Ashok K. Bhargava * Elizabeth Castillo * Swapna Behera
Tezmin Ition Tsai * William S. Peters, Sr.

Now Available

www.innerchildpress.com/the-year-of-the-poet

The Year of the Poet VIII
September 2021
Featured Global Poets
Monsif Beroual * Sandesh Ghimire
Sharmila Poudel * Pavol Janik

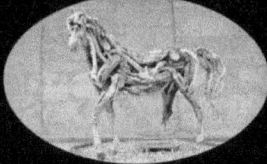

Heather Jansch

Poetry . . . Ekphrasticly Speaking

The Poetry Posse 2021
Gail Weston Shazor * Albert Carasco * Hülya N. Yılmaz
Jackie Davis Allen * Caroline Nazareno * Eliza Segiet
Alicja Maria Kuberska * Teresa E. Gallion * Joe Paire
Kimberly Burnham * Shareef Abdur – Rasheed
Ashok K. Bhargava * Elizabeth Castillo * Swapna Behera
Tezmin Ition Tsai * William S. Peters, Sr.

The Year of the Poet VIII
October 2021
Featured Global Poets
C. E. Shy * Saswata Ganguly
Suranjit Gain * Hasiba Hilal

Dale Lamphere

Poetry . . . Ekphrasticly Speaking

The Poetry Posse 2021
Gail Weston Shazor * Albert Carasco * Hülya N. Yılmaz
Jackie Davis Allen * Caroline Nazareno * Eliza Segiet
Alicja Maria Kuberska * Teresa E. Gallion * Joe Paire
Kimberly Burnham * Shareef Abdur – Rasheed
Ashok K. Bhargava * Elizabeth Castillo * Swapna Behera
Tezmin Ition Tsai * William S. Peters, Sr.

The Year of the Poet VIII
November 2021
Featured Global Poets
Errol D. Bean * Ibrahim Honjo
Tanja Ajtic * Rajashree Mohapatra

Andy Goldsworthy

Poetry . . . Ekphrasticly Speaking

The Poetry Posse 2021
Gail Weston Shazor * Albert Carasco * Hülya N. Yılmaz
Jackie Davis Allen * Caroline Nazareno * Eliza Segiet
Alicja Maria Kuberska * Teresa E. Gallion * Joe Paire
Kimberly Burnham * Shareef Abdur – Rasheed
Ashok K. Bhargava * Elizabeth Castillo * Swapna Behera
Tezmin Ition Tsai * William S. Peters, Sr.

The Year of the Poet VIII
December 2021
Featured Global Poets
Orbinda Ganga * Fadairo Tesleem
Anthony Arnold * Iyad Shamasnah

Fredric Edwin Church

Poetry . . . Ekphrasticly Speaking

The Poetry Posse 2021
Gail Weston Shazor * Albert Carasco * Hülya N. Yılmaz
Jackie Davis Allen * Caroline Nazareno * Eliza Segiet
Alicja Maria Kuberska * Teresa E. Gallion * Joe Paire
Kimberly Burnham * Shareef Abdur – Rasheed
Ashok K. Bhargava * Elizabeth Castillo * Swapna Behera
Tezmin Ition Tsai * William S. Peters, Sr.

Now Available

www.innerchildpress.com/the-year-of-the-poet

The Year of the Poet IX
January 2022

Featured Global Poets
**Ratan Ghosh * Christine Neil-Wright
Andrew Scott * Ashok Kumar**

Climate Change : The Ice Cap

Poetry . . . Ekphrasticly Speaking

The Poetry Posse 2021

Gail Weston Shazor * Albert Carasco * Hülya N. Yılmaz
Jackie Davis Allen * Caroline Nazareno * Eliza Segiet
Alicja Maria Kuberska * Teresa E. Gallion * Joe Paire
Kimberly Burnham * Shareef Abdur – Rasheed
Ashok K. Bhargava * Elizabeth Castillo * Swapna Behera
Tezmin Ition Tsai * William S. Peters, Sr.

The Year of the Poet IX
February 2022

Featured Global Poets
Roza Boyanova * Ramón de Jesús Núñez Duval
Mammad Ismayil * Tarana Turan Rahimli

Climate Change and Mountains

Poetry . . . Ekphrasticly Speaking

The Poetry Posse 2021

Gail Weston Shazor * Albert Carasco * Hülya N. Yılmaz
Jackie Davis Allen * Caroline Nazareno * Eliza Segiet
Alicja Maria Kuberska * Teresa E. Gallion * Joe Paire
Kimberly Burnham * Shareef Abdur – Rasheed
Ashok K. Bhargava * Elizabeth Castillo * Swapna Behera
Tezmin Ition Tsai * William S. Peters, Sr.

The Year of the Poet IX
March 2022

Featured Global Poets
Dimitris P. Kraniotis * Marlene Pasini
Kennedy Ochieng * Swayam Prashant

Climate Change and Space Debris

Poetry . . . Ekphrasticly Speaking

The Poetry Posse 2021

Gail Weston Shazor * Albert Carasco * Hülya N. Yılmaz
Jackie Davis Allen * Caroline Nazareno * Eliza Segiet
Alicja Maria Kuberska * Teresa E. Gallion * Joe Paire
Kimberly Burnham * Shareef Abdur – Rasheed
Ashok K. Bhargava * Elizabeth Castillo * Swapna Behera
Tezmin Ition Tsai * William S. Peters, Sr.

The Year of the Poet IX
April 2022

Featured Global Poets
**Alonzo Gross * Dr. Debaprasanna Biswas
Monsif Beroual * Carol Aronoff**

Climate Change and Oceans

*Celebrating our 100th Edition *

Poetry . . . Ekphrasticly Speaking

The Poetry Posse 2021

Gail Weston Shazor * Albert Carasco * Hülya N. Yılmaz
Jackie Davis Allen * Caroline Nazareno * Eliza Segiet
Alicja Maria Kuberska * Teresa E. Gallion * Joe Paire
Kimberly Burnham * Shareef Abdur – Rasheed
Ashok K. Bhargava * Elizabeth Castillo * Swapna Behera
Tezmin Ition Tsai * William S. Peters, Sr.

Now Available

www.innerchildpress.com/the-year-of-the-poet

The Year of the Poet IX
May 2022

Featured Global Poets

Ndaba Sibanda * Smrutiranjan Mohanty
Ajanta Paul * Monalisa Dash Dwibedy

Climate Change and Birds

Poetry . . . Ekphrasticly Speaking

The Poetry Posse 2021

Gail Weston Shazor * Albert Carasco * Hülya N. Yılmaz
Jackie Davis Allen * Caroline Nazareno * Eliza Segiet
Alicja Maria Kuberska * Teresa E. Gallion * Joe Paire
Kimberly Burnham * Shareef Abdur – Rasheed
Ashok K. Bhargava * Elizabeth Castillo * Swapna Behera
Tezmin Ition Tsai * William S. Peters, Sr.

The Year of the Poet IX
June 2022

Featured Global Poets

Yuan Changming * Azeezat Okunlola
Tanja Ajtić * Philip Chijioke Abonyi

Climate Change and Trees

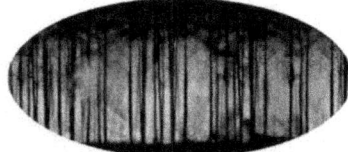

Poetry . . . Ekphrasticly Speaking

The Poetry Posse 2022

Gail Weston Shazor * Albert Carasco * Hülya N. Yılmaz
Jackie Davis Allen * Caroline Nazareno * Eliza Segiet
Alicja Maria Kuberska * Teresa E. Gallion * Joe Paire
Kimberly Burnham * Shareef Abdur – Rasheed
Ashok K. Bhargava * Elizabeth Castillo * Swapna Behera
Tezmin Ition Tsai * William S. Peters, Sr.

The Year of the Poet IX
July 2022

Featured Global Poets

Michelle Joan Barulich * Mili Das
Anna Ferriero * Ujjal Mandal

Climate Change and Animals

Poetry . . . Ekphrasticly Speaking

The Poetry Posse 2022

Gail Weston Shazor * Albert Carasco * Hülya N. Yılmaz
Jackie Davis Allen * Caroline Nazareno * Eliza Segiet
Alicja Maria Kuberska * Teresa E. Gallion * Joe Paire
Kimberly Burnham * Shareef Abdur – Rasheed
Ashok K. Bhargava * Elizabeth Castillo * Swapna Behera
Tezmin Ition Tsai * William S. Peters, Sr.

The Year of the Poet IX
August 2022

Featured Global Poets

Pankhuri Sinha * Abdulloh Abdumominov
Caroline Turunç * Tali Cohen Shabtai

Climate Change and Agriculture

Poetry . . . Ekphrasticly Speaking

The Poetry Posse 2022

Gail Weston Shazor * Albert Carasco * Hülya N. Yılmaz
Jackie Davis Allen * Caroline Nazareno * Eliza Segiet
Alicja Maria Kuberska * Teresa E. Gallion * Joe Paire
Kimberly Burnham * Shareef Abdur – Rasheed
Ashok K. Bhargava * Elizabeth Castillo * Swapna Behera
Tezmin Ition Tsai * William S. Peters, Sr.

Now Available

www.innerchildpress.com/the-year-of-the-poet

The Year of the Poet IX
September 2022

Featured Global Poets
Ngozi Olivia Osuoha * Biswajit Mishra
Sylwia K. Malinowska * Sajid Hussein

Climate Change and Wind and Weather Patterns

Poetry ... Ekphrasticly Speaking

The Poetry Posse 2022

Gail Weston Shazor * Albert Carasco * Hülya N. Yılmaz
Jackie Davis Allen * Caroline Nazareno * Eliza Segiet
Alicja Maria Kuberska * Teresa E. Gallion * Joe Paire
Kimberly Burnham * Shareef Abdur – Rasheed
Ashok K. Bhargava * Elizabeth Castillo * Swapna Behera
Tezmin Ition Tsai * William S. Peters, Sr.

The Year of the Poet IX
October 2022

Featured Global Poets
Andrew Kouroupos * Brenda Mohammed
Carthornia Kouroupos * Faleeha Hassan

Climate Change and Oil and Power

Poetry ... Ekphrasticly Speaking

The Poetry Posse 2022

Gail Weston Shazor * Albert Carasco * Hülya N. Yılmaz
Jackie Davis Allen * Caroline Nazareno * Eliza Segiet
Alicja Maria Kuberska * Teresa E. Gallion * Joe Paire
Kimberly Burnham * Shareef Abdur – Rasheed
Ashok K. Bhargava * Elizabeth Castillo * Swapna Behera
Tezmin Ition Tsai * William S. Peters, Sr.

The Year of the Poet IX
November 2022

Featured Global Poets
Hema Ravi * Shafkat Aziz Hajam
Selma Kopic * Ibrahim Honjo

Climate Change : Time to Act

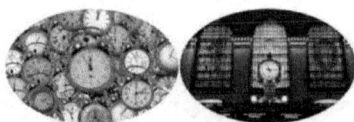

Poetry ... Ekphrasticly Speaking

The Poetry Posse 2022

Gail Weston Shazor * Albert Carasco * Hülya N. Yılmaz
Jackie Davis Allen * Caroline Nazareno * Eliza Segiet
Alicja Maria Kuberska * Teresa E. Gallion * Joe Paire
Kimberly Burnham * Shareef Abdur – Rasheed
Ashok K. Bhargava * Elizabeth Castillo * Swapna Behera
Tezmin Ition Tsai * William S. Peters, Sr.

The Year of the Poet IX
December 2022

Featured Global Poets
Elarbi Abdelfattah * Lorraine Cragg
Neha Bhandarkar * Robert Gibbons

Climate Change Bees, Butterflies and Insect Life

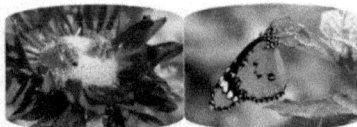

Poetry ... Ekphrasticly Speaking

The Poetry Posse 2022

Gail Weston Shazor * Albert Carasco * Hülya N. Yılmaz
Jackie Davis Allen * Caroline Nazareno * Eliza Segiet
Alicja Maria Kuberska * Teresa E. Gallion * Joe Paire
Kimberly Burnham * Shareef Abdur – Rasheed
Ashok K. Bhargava * Elizabeth Castillo * Swapna Behera
Tezmin Ition Tsai * William S. Peters, Sr.

Now Available

www.innerchildpress.com/the-year-of-the-poet

The Year of the Poet X
January 2023

Featured Global Poets

JuNe Barefield * Swayam Prashant
Willow Rose * Shabbirhusein K Jamnagerwalla

Children : Difference Makers

Iqbal Masih

The Poetry Posse 2023

Gail Weston Shazor * Albert Carasco * Hülya N. Yılmaz
Jackie Davis Allen * Caroline Nazareno * Kimberly Burnham
Alicja Maria Kuberska * Teresa E. Gallion * Joe Paire
Michelle Joan Barulich * Shareef Abdur – Rasheed
Ashok K. Bhargava * Elizabeth Castillo * Swapna Behera
Tezmin Ition Tsai * Eliza Segiet * William S. Peters, Sr.

The Year of the Poet X
February 2023

Featured Global Poets

Christena Williams * Hilda Graciela Kraft
Francesco Favetta * Dr. H.C. Louise Hudon

Children : Difference Makers

Ruby Bridges

The Poetry Posse 2023

Gail Weston Shazor * Albert Carasco * Hülya N. Yılmaz
Jackie Davis Allen * Caroline Nazareno * Kimberly Burnham
Alicja Maria Kuberska * Teresa E. Gallion * Joe Paire
Michelle Joan Barulich * Shareef Abdur – Rasheed
Ashok K. Bhargava * Elizabeth Castillo * Swapna Behera
Tezmin Ition Tsai * Eliza Segiet * William S. Peters, Sr.

The Year of the Poet X
March 2023

Featured Global Poets

Clarena Martinez Turizo * Binod Dawadi
Til Kumari Sharma * Petrouchka Alexieva

Children : Difference Makers

Yo Yo Ma

The Poetry Posse 2023

Gail Weston Shazor * Albert Carasco * Hülya N. Yılmaz
Jackie Davis Allen * Caroline Nazareno * Kimberly Burnham
Alicja Maria Kuberska * Teresa E. Gallion * Joe Paire
Michelle Joan Barulich * Shareef Abdur – Rasheed
Ashok K. Bhargava * Elizabeth Castillo * Swapna Behera
Tezmin Ition Tsai * Eliza Segiet * William S. Peters, Sr.

The Year of the Poet X
April 2023

Featured Global Poets

Maxwanette A Poetess * Alonzo Gross
Türkan Ergör * Ibrahim Honjo

Children : Difference Makers

Claudette Colvin

The Poetry Posse 2023

Gail Weston Shazor * Albert Carasco * Hülya N. Yılmaz
Jackie Davis Allen * Caroline Nazareno * Kimberly Burnham
Alicja Maria Kuberska * Teresa E. Gallion * Joe Paire
Michelle Joan Barulich * Shareef Abdur – Rasheed
Ashok K. Bhargava * Elizabeth Castillo * Swapna Behera
Tezmin Ition Tsai * Eliza Segiet * William S. Peters, Sr.

Now Available

www.innerchildpress.com/the-year-of-the-poet

The Year of the Poet X
May 2023

Csp Shrivastava * Michael Lee Johnson
Taghrid Bou Merhi * Yasmin Brown

Children : Difference Makers

Louis Braille

The Poetry Posse 2023

Gail Weston Shazor * Albert Carasco * Hülya N. Yılmaz
Jackie Davis Allen * Caroline Nazareno * Kimberly Burnham
Alicja Maria Kuberska * Teresa E. Gallion * Joe Paire
Michelle Joan Barulich * Shareef Abdur – Rasheed
Ashok K. Bhargava * Elizabeth Castillo * Swapna Behera
Tezmin Ition Tsai * Eliza Segiet * William S. Peters, Sr.

The Year of the Poet X
June 2023

Featured Global Poets

Kay Peters   Carthornia Kouroupos
Andrew Kouroupos   Faleeha Hassan

Children : Difference Makers

Ryan Hreljac

The Poetry Posse 2023

The Year of the Poet X
July 2023

Featured Global Poets

Rajashree Mohapatra * Biswajit Mishra
Johan Karlsson * Teodozja Świderska

Children : Difference Makers

~ Bana al-Abed ~

The Poetry Posse 2023

Gail Weston Shazor * Albert Carasco * Hülya N. Yılmaz
Jackie Davis Allen * Caroline Nazareno * Kimberly Burnham
Alicja Maria Kuberska * Teresa E. Gallion * Joe Paire
Michelle Joan Barulich * Shareef Abdur – Rasheed
Ashok K. Bhargava * Elizabeth Castillo * Swapna Behera
Tezmin Ition Tsai * Eliza Segiet * William S. Peters, Sr.

The Year of the Poet X
August 2023

Featured Global Poets

Kennedy Wanda Ochieng * Jose Lopez
Sylwia K. Malinowska * Laurent Grison

Children : Difference Makers

~ Kelvin Doe ~

The Poetry Posse 2023

Gail Weston Shazor * Albert Carasco * Hülya N. Yılmaz
Jackie Davis Allen * Caroline Nazareno * Kimberly Burnham
Alicja Maria Kuberska * Teresa E. Gallion * Joe Paire
Michelle Joan Barulich * Shareef Abdur – Rasheed
Ashok K. Bhargava * Elizabeth Castillo * Swapna Behera
Tezmin Ition Tsai * Eliza Segiet * William S. Peters, Sr.

Now Available

www.innerchildpress.com/the-year-of-the-poet

The Year of the Poet X
September 2023

Featured Global Poets

Eftichia Karpadeli * Chinh Nguyen
Nigar Agalarova * Carmela Cueva

Children : Difference Makers

~ Easton LaChappelle ~

The Poetry Posse 2023

Gail Weston Shazor * Albert Carassco * Hülya N. Yılmaz
Jackie Davis Allen * Caroline Nazareno * Kimberly Burnham
Alicja Maria Kuberska * Teresa E. Gallion * Joe Paire
Michelle Joan Barulich * Shareef Abdur – Rasheed
Ashok K. Bhargava * Elizabeth Castillo * Swapna Behera
Tezmin Ition Tsai * Eliza Segiet * William S. Peters, Sr.

The Year of the Poet X
October 2023

Featured Global Poets

CSP Shrivastava * Huniie Parker
Noreen Snyder * Ramkrishna Paul

Children : Difference Makers

~ Malala Yousafzai ~

The Poetry Posse 2023

Gail Weston Shazor * Albert Carassco * Hülya N. Yılmaz
Jackie Davis Allen * Caroline Nazareno * Kimberly Burnham
Alicja Maria Kuberska * Teresa E. Gallion * Joe Paire
Michelle Joan Barulich * Shareef Abdur – Rasheed
Ashok K. Bhargava * Elizabeth Castillo * Swapna Behera
Tezmin Ition Tsai * Eliza Segiet * William S. Peters, Sr.

The Year of the Poet X
November 2023

Featured Global Poets

Ibrahim Honjo * Balachandran Nair
Xanthi Hondrou-Hil * Francesco Favetta

Children : Difference Makers

~ Jean-Michel Basquiat ~

The Poetry Posse 2023

Gail Weston Shazor * Albert Carassco * Hülya N. Yılmaz
Jackie Davis Allen * Caroline Nazareno * Kimberly Burnham
Alicja Maria Kuberska * Teresa E. Gallion * Joe Paire
Michelle Joan Barulich * Shareef Abdur – Rasheed
Ashok K. Bhargava * Elizabeth Castillo * Swapna Behera
Tezmin Ition Tsai * Eliza Segiet * William S. Peters, Sr.

The Year of the Poet X
December 2023

Featured Global Poets

Caroline Laurent Turunc * Neha Bhandarkar
Shafkat Aziz Hajam * Elarbi Abdelfattah

Children : Difference Makers

~ Melati and Isabel Wijsen ~

The Poetry Posse 2023

Gail Weston Shazor * Albert Carassco * Hülya N. Yılmaz
Jackie Davis Allen * Caroline Nazareno * Kimberly Burnham
Alicja Maria Kuberska * Teresa E. Gallion * Joe Paire
Michelle Joan Barulich * Shareef Abdur – Rasheed
Ashok K. Bhargava * Elizabeth Castillo * Swapna Behera
Tezmin Ition Tsai * Eliza Segiet * William S. Peters, Sr.

Now Available

www.innerchildpress.com/the-year-of-the-poet

The Year of the Poet XI
January 2024

Featured Global Poets

Til Kumari Sharma * Shafkat Aziz Hajam
Daniela Marian * Eleni Vassiliou - Asteroskon

Renowned Poets

~ Phyllis Wheatley ~

The Poetry Posse 2024

Gail Weston Shazor * Albert Carasco * Hülya N. Yılmaz
Jackie Davis Allen * Caroline Nazareno * Mutawaf Shaheed
Alicja Maria Kuberska * Teresa E. Gallion * Noreen Snyder
Michelle Joan Barulich * Shareef Abdur – Rasheed
Ashok K. Bhargava * Elizabeth Castillo * Swapna Behera
Tezmin Ition Tsai * Eliza Segiet * William S. Peters, Sr.

The Year of the Poet XI
February 2024

Featured Global Poets

Caroline Laurent Turunç * Julio Pavanetti
Lidia Chiarelli * Lina Buividavičiūtė

Renowned Poets

~ Omar Khayyam ~

The Poetry Posse 2024

Gail Weston Shazor * Albert Carasco * Hülya N. Yılmaz
Jackie Davis Allen * Caroline Nazareno * Mutawaf Shaheed
Alicja Maria Kuberska * Teresa E. Gallion * Noreen Snyder
Michelle Joan Barulich * Shareef Abdur – Rasheed
Ashok K. Bhargava * Elizabeth Castillo * Swapna Behera
Tezmin Ition Tsai * Eliza Segiet * William S. Peters, Sr.

The Year of the Poet XI
March 2024

Featured Global Poets

Francesco Favetta * Jagjit Singh Zandu
Carmela Nûñez Yukimura Peruana * Michael Lee Johnson

Renowned Poets

~ Nâzim Hikmet ~

The Poetry Posse 2024

Gail Weston Shazor * Albert Carasco * Hülya N. Yılmaz
Jackie Davis Allen * Caroline Nazareno * Mutawaf Shaheed
Alicja Maria Kuberska * Teresa E. Gallion * Noreen Snyder
Michelle Joan Barulich * Shareef Abdur – Rasheed
Ashok K. Bhargava * Elizabeth Castillo * Swapna Behera
Tezmin Ition Tsai * Eliza Segiet * William S. Peters, Sr.

The Year of the Poet XI
April 2024

Featured Global Poets

Hassanal Abdullah * Johny Takkedasila
Rajashree Mohapatra * Shirley Smothers

Renowned Poets

~ William Butler Yeats ~

The Poetry Posse 2024

Gail Weston Shazor * Albert Carasco * Hülya N. Yılmaz
Jackie Davis Allen * Caroline Nazareno * Mutawaf Shaheed
Alicja Maria Kuberska * Teresa E. Gallion * Noreen Snyder
Michelle Joan Barulich * Shareef Abdur – Rasheed
Ashok K. Bhargava * Elizabeth Castillo * Swapna Behera
Tezmin Ition Tsai * Eliza Segiet * William S. Peters, Sr.

Now Available

www.innerchildpress.com/the-year-of-the-poet

The Year of the Poet XI
May 2024

Featured Global Poets

Binod Dawadi * Petros Kyriakou Veloudas
Rayees Ahmad Kumar * Solomon C Jatta

Renowned Poets

~ Makhanlal Chaturvedi ~

The Poetry Posse 2024

Gail Weston Shazor * Albert Carasco * Hülya N. Yılmaz
Jackie Davis Allen * Caroline Nazareno * Mutawaf Shaheed
Alicja Maria Kuberska * Teresa E. Gallion * Noreen Snyder
Michelle Joan Barulich * Shareef Abdur – Rasheed
Ashok K. Bhargava * Elizabeth Castillo * Swapna Behera
Tezmin Ition Tsai * Eliza Segiet * William S. Peters, Sr.

The Year of the Poet XI
June 2024

Featured Global Poets

C. S. P Shrivastava * Maria Evelyn Quilla Soleta
Moulay Cherif Chebihi Hassani * Swayam Prashant

Renowned Poets

~ Langston Hughs ~

The Poetry Posse 2024

Gail Weston Shazor * Albert Carasco * Hülya N. Yılmaz
Jackie Davis Allen * Caroline Nazareno * Mutawaf Shaheed
Alicja Maria Kuberska * Teresa E. Gallion * Noreen Snyder
Michelle Joan Barulich * Shareef Abdur – Rasheed
Ashok K. Bhargava * Elizabeth Castillo * Swapna Behera
Tezmin Ition Tsai * Eliza Segiet * William S. Peters, Sr.

The Year of the Poet XI
July 2024

Featured Global Poets

Barbara Gaiardoni * Bharati Nayak
Errol Bean * Michael Lee Johnson

Renowned Poets

~ Pablo Neruda ~

The Poetry Posse 2024

Gail Weston Shazor * Albert Carasco * Hülya N. Yılmaz
Jackie Davis Allen * Caroline Nazareno * Mutawaf Shaheed
Alicja Maria Kuberska * Teresa E. Gallion * Noreen Snyder
Michelle Joan Barulich * Shareef Abdur – Rasheed
Ashok K. Bhargava * Elizabeth Castillo * Swapna Behera
Tezmin Ition Tsai * Eliza Segiet * William S. Peters, Sr.

The Year of the Poet XI
August 2024

Featured Global Poets

Ibrahim Honjo * Khalice Jade
Irma Kurti * Mennadi Farah

Renowned Poets

~ Li Bai ~

The Poetry Posse 2024

Gail Weston Shazor * Albert Carasco * Hülya N. Yılmaz
Jackie Davis Allen * Caroline Nazareno * Mutawaf Shaheed
Alicja Maria Kuberska * Teresa E. Gallion * Noreen Snyder
Michelle Joan Barulich * Shareef Abdur – Rasheed
Ashok K. Bhargava * Elizabeth Castillo * Swapna Behera
Tezmin Ition Tsai * Eliza Segiet * William S. Peters, Sr.

Now Available

www.innerchildpress.com/the-year-of-the-poet

The Year of the Poet XI
September 2024

Featured Global Poets

Ngozi Olivia Osuoha * Teodozja Świderska
Chinh Nguyen * Awatef El Idrissi Boukhris

Renowned Poets

~ William Ernest Henley ~

The Poetry Posse 2024

Gail Weston Shazor * Albert Carasco * Hülya N. Yılmaz
Jackie Davis Allen * Caroline Nazareno * Mutawaf Shaheed
Alicja Maria Kuberska * Teresa E. Gallion * Noreen Snyder
Michelle Joan Barulich * Shareef Abdur – Rasheed
Ashok K. Bhargava * Elizabeth Castillo * Swapna Behera
Tezmin Ition Tsai * Eliza Segiet * William S. Peters, Sr.

The Year of the Poet XI
October 2024

Featured Global Poets

Deepak Kumar Dey * Shallal 'Anouz
Adnan Al-Sayegh * Taghrid Bou Merhi

Renowned Poets

~ Adam Mickiewicz ~

The Poetry Posse 2024

Gail Weston Shazor * Albert Carasco * Hülya N. Yılmaz
Jackie Davis Allen * Caroline Nazareno * Mutawaf Shaheed
Alicja Maria Kuberska * Teresa E. Gallion * Noreen Snyder
Michelle Joan Barulich * Shareef Abdur – Rasheed
Ashok K. Bhargava * Elizabeth Castillo * Swapna Behera
Tezmin Ition Tsai * Eliza Segiet * William S. Peters, Sr.

The Year of the Poet XI
November 2024

Featured Global Poets

Abraham Tawiah Tei * Neha Bhandarkar
Zaneta Varnado Johns * Haseena Bnaiyan

Renowned Poets

~ Wole Soyinka ~

The Poetry Posse 2024

Gail Weston Shazor * Albert Carasco * Hülya N. Yılmaz
Jackie Davis Allen * Caroline Nazareno * Mutawaf Shaheed
Alicja Maria Kuberska * Teresa E. Gallion * Noreen Snyder
Michelle Joan Barulich * Shareef Abdur – Rasheed
Ashok K. Bhargava * Elizabeth Castillo * Swapna Behera
Tezmin Ition Tsai * Eliza Segiet * William S. Peters, Sr.

The Year of the Poet XI
December 2024

Featured Global Poets

Kapardeli Eftichia * Irena Jovanović
Sudipta Mishra * Til Kumari Sharma

Renowned Poets

~ Imru' al-Qais ~

The Poetry Posse 2024

Gail Weston Shazor * Albert Carasco * Hülya N. Yılmaz
Jackie Davis Allen * Caroline Nazareno * Mutawaf Shaheed
Alicja Maria Kuberska * Teresa E. Gallion * Noreen Snyder
Michelle Joan Barulich * Shareef Abdur – Rasheed
Ashok K. Bhargava * Elizabeth Castillo * Kimberly Burnham
Tezmin Ition Tsai * Eliza Segiet * William S. Peters, Sr.

Now Available

www.innerchildpress.com/the-year-of-the-poet

and there is much, much more !

visit . . .

www.innerchildpress.com/antho
logies-sales-special.php

Also check out our Authors and
all the wonderful Books
Available at :

www.innerchildpress.com/autho
rs-pages

World Healing World Peace
2020

Poets for Humanity

Now Available

www.worldhealingworldpeacepoetry.com

Now Available

www.worldhealingworldpeacepoetry.com

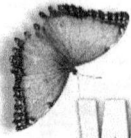

I support World Healing World Peace

www.worldhealingworldpeacepoetry.com

World Healing World Peace logo — "World Healing World Peace" arched around "PoEtRy" with "i am a believer!" beneath

World Healing
World Peace

2012, 2014, 2016, 2018, 2020, 2022

Now Available

www.worldhealingworldpeacepoetry.com

254

Inner Child Press International

'building bridges of cultural understanding'

Meet our Cultural Ambassadors

Fahredin Shehu
Director of Cultural

Faleha Hassan
Iraq – USA

Elizabeth E. Castillo
Philippines

Antoinette Coleman
Chicago
Midwest USA

Ananda Nepali
Nepal – Tibet
Northern India

Kimberly Burnham
Pacific Northwest
USA

Alicja Kuberska
Poland
Eastern Europe

Swapna Behera
India
Southeast Asia

Kolade O. Freedom
Nigeria
West Africa

Monsif Beroual
Morocco
Northern Africa

Ashok K. Bhargava
Canada

Tzemin Ition Tsai
Republic of China
Greater China

Alicia M. Ramírez
Mexico
Central America

Christena AV Williams
Jamaica
Caribbean

Louise Hudon
Eastern Canada

Aziz Mountassir
Morocco
Northern Africa

Shareef Abdur-Rasheed
Southeastern USA

Laure Charazac
France
Western Europe

Mohammad Ikbal Harb
Lebanon
Middle East

Mohamed Abdel Aziz Shmeis
Egypt
Middle East

Hilary Mainga
Kenya
Eastern Africa

Josephus R. Johnson
Liberia

Mennadi Farah
Algeria

www.innerchildpress.com

This Anthological Publication
is underwritten solely by

Inner Child Press International

Inner Child Press is a Publishing Company
Founded and Operated by Writers. Our
personal publishing experiences provides
us an intimate understanding of the
sometimes daunting challenges Writers,
New and Seasoned may face in the
Business of Publishing and Marketing
their Creative "Written Work".

For more Information

Inner Child Press International

www.innerchildpress.com

Inner Child Press International

'building bridges of cultural understanding'

202 Wiltree Court, State College, Pennsylvania 16801

www.innerchildpress.com

~ fini ~

www.ingramcontent.com/pod-product-compliance
Lightning Source LLC
LaVergne TN
LVHW051041080426
835508LV00019B/1639